this BOOK
BeLONGS tO

____

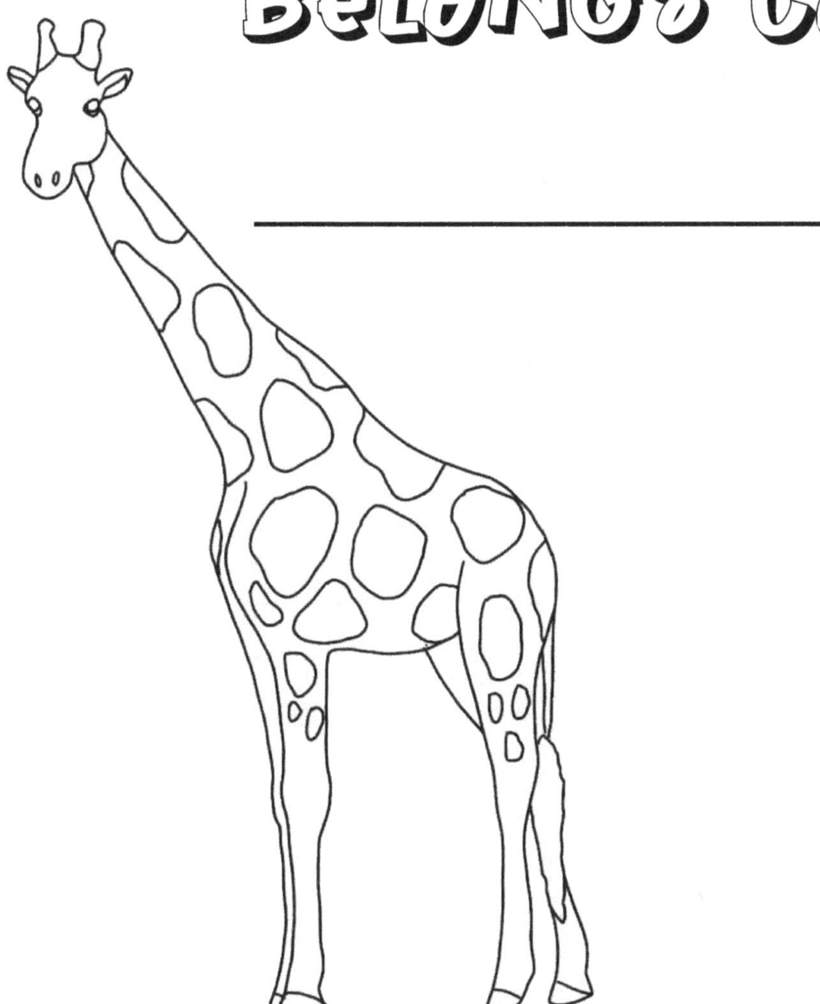

More coloring books styles & artwork at

amazon.com/author/jillharmony

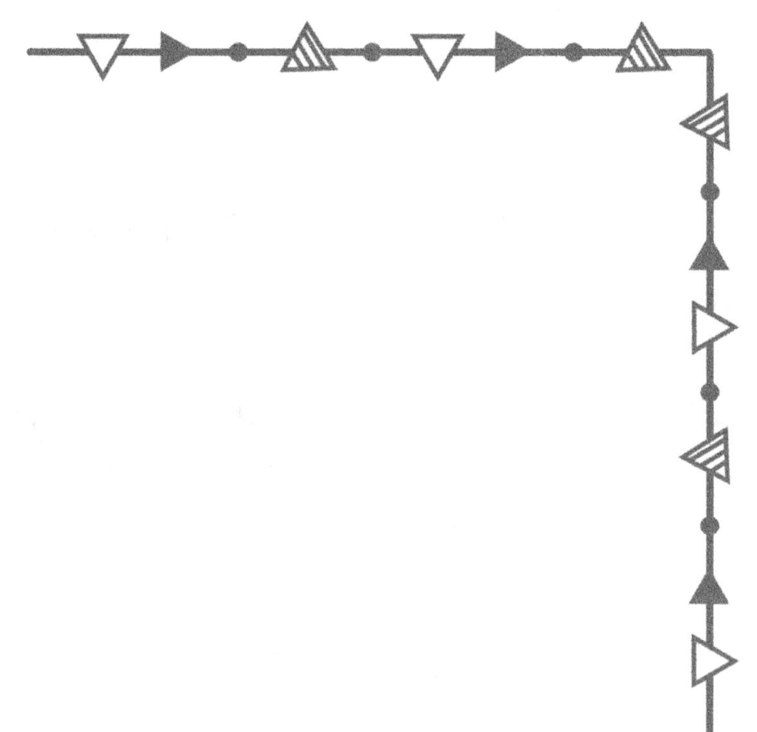
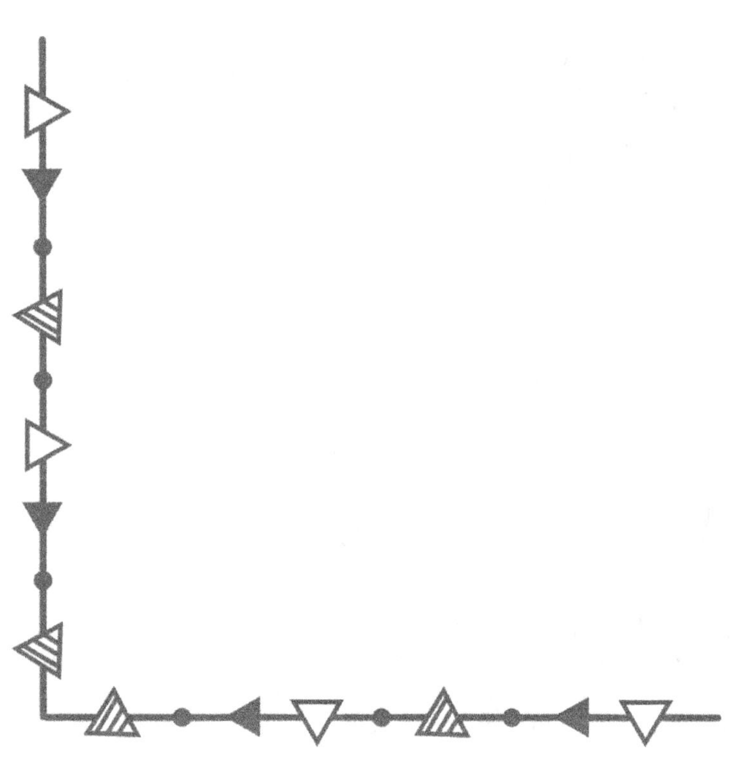

Pretty
as a
peacock

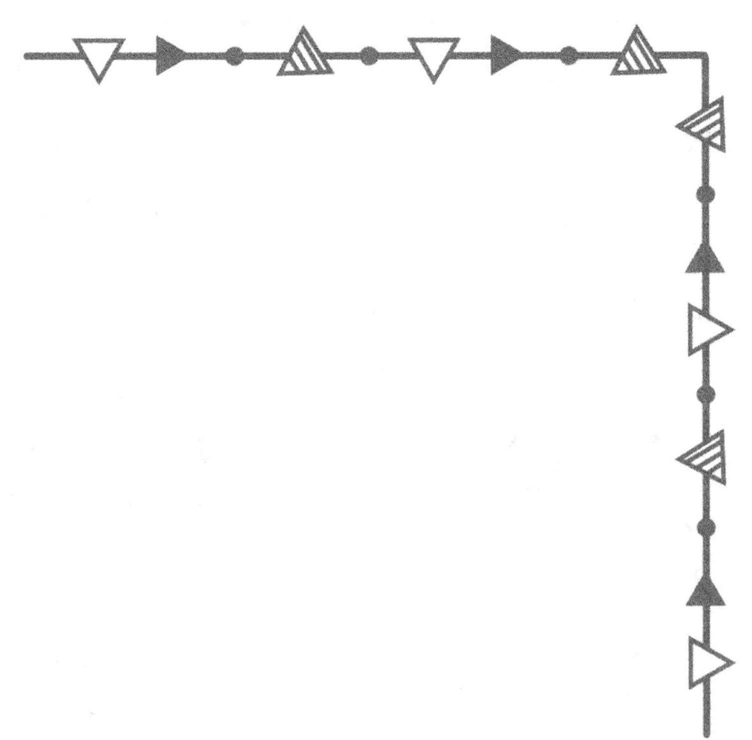
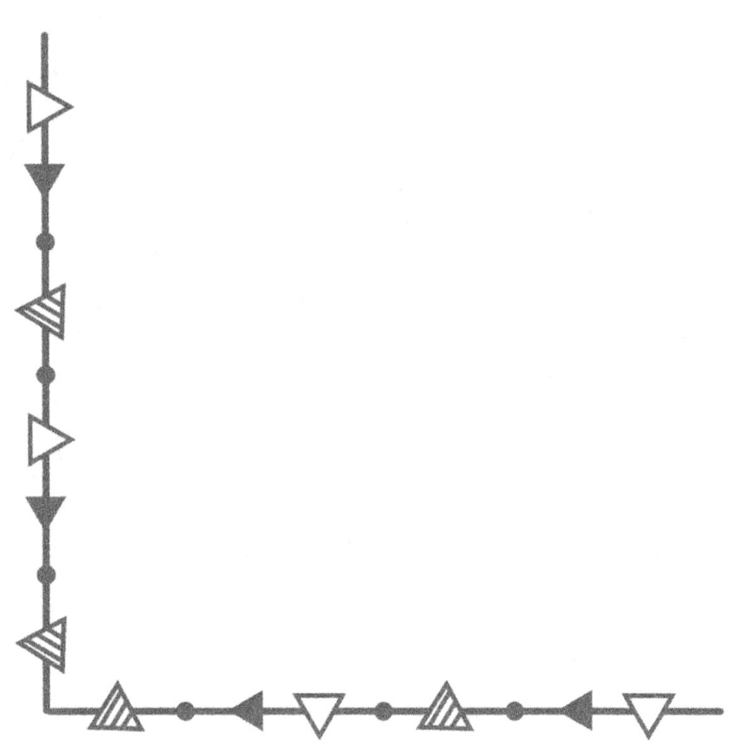

TALL AS A
GIRAFFE

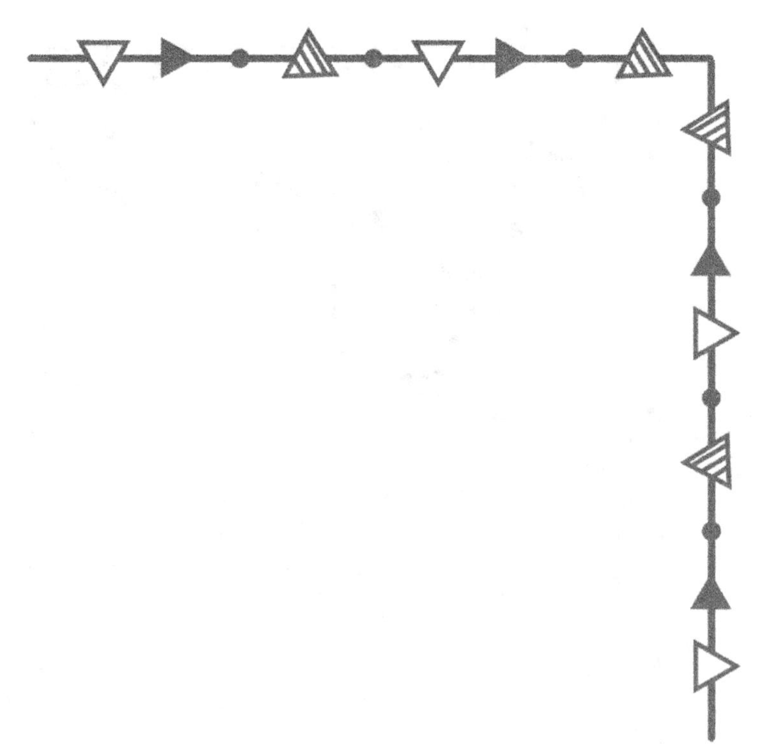

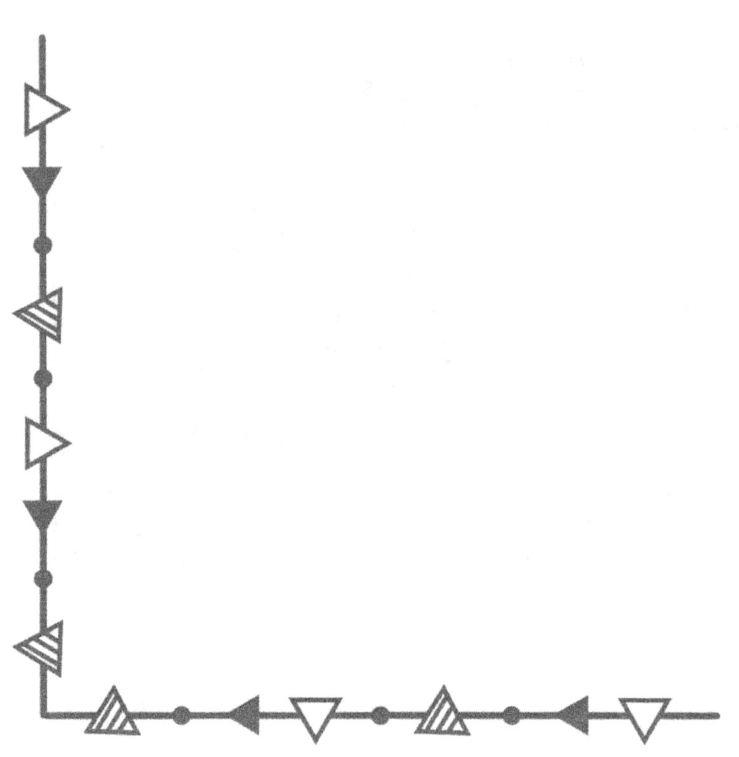

REGAL
AS AN
EAGLE

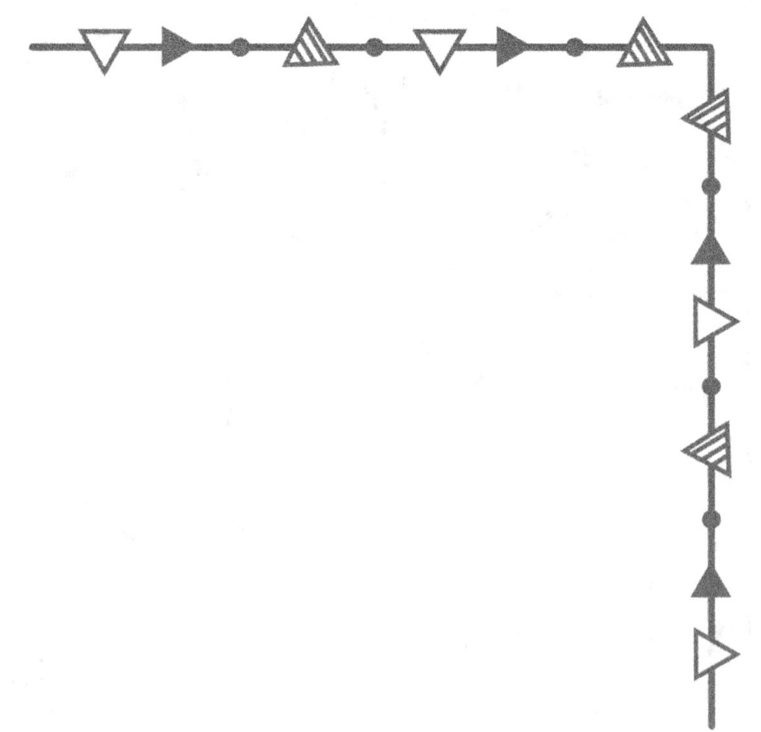
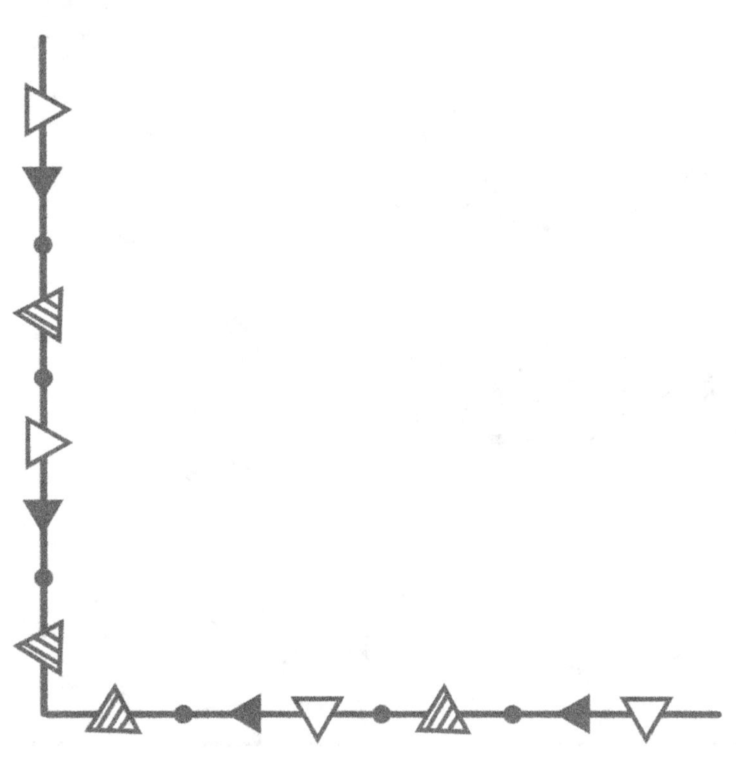

Happy
as a
clam

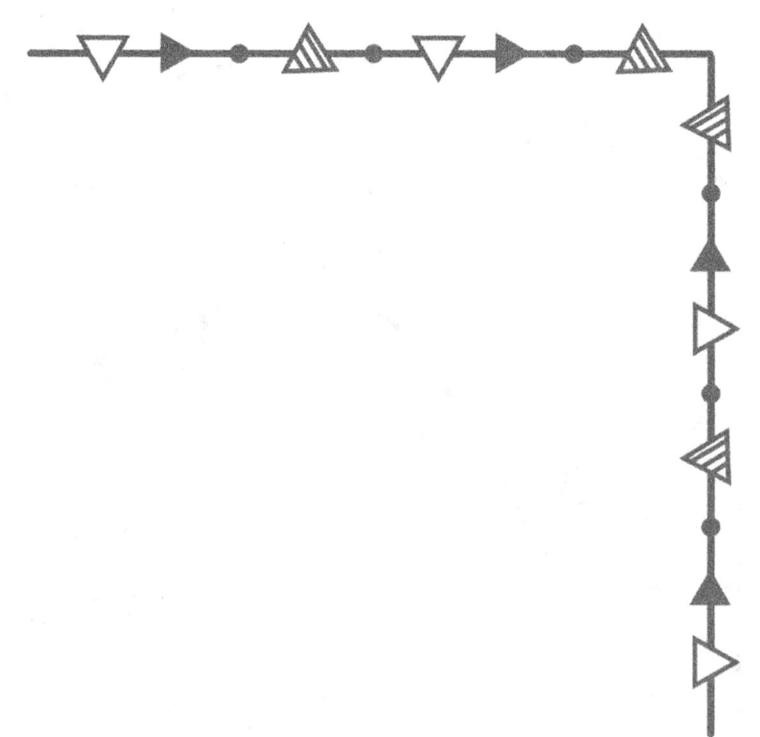

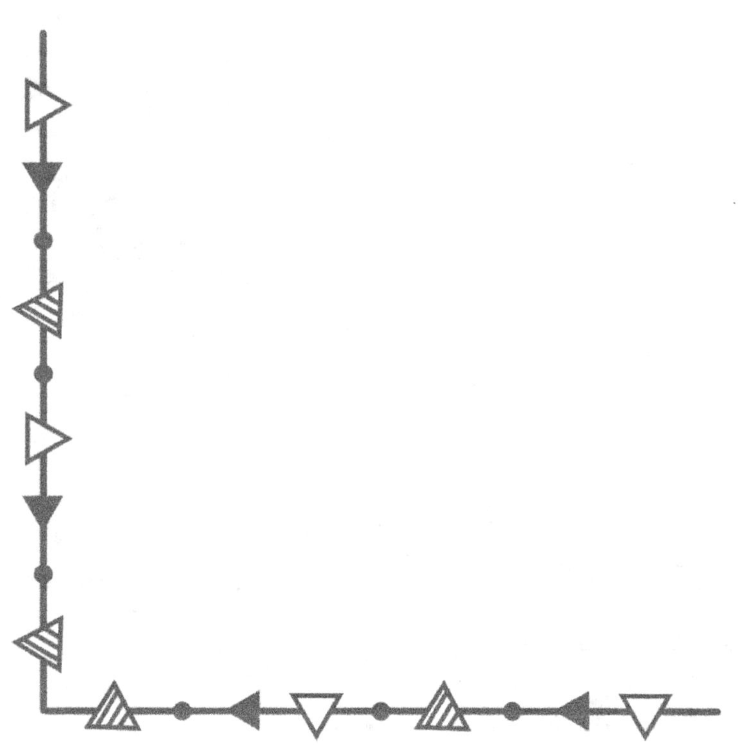

sleek
as a
cat

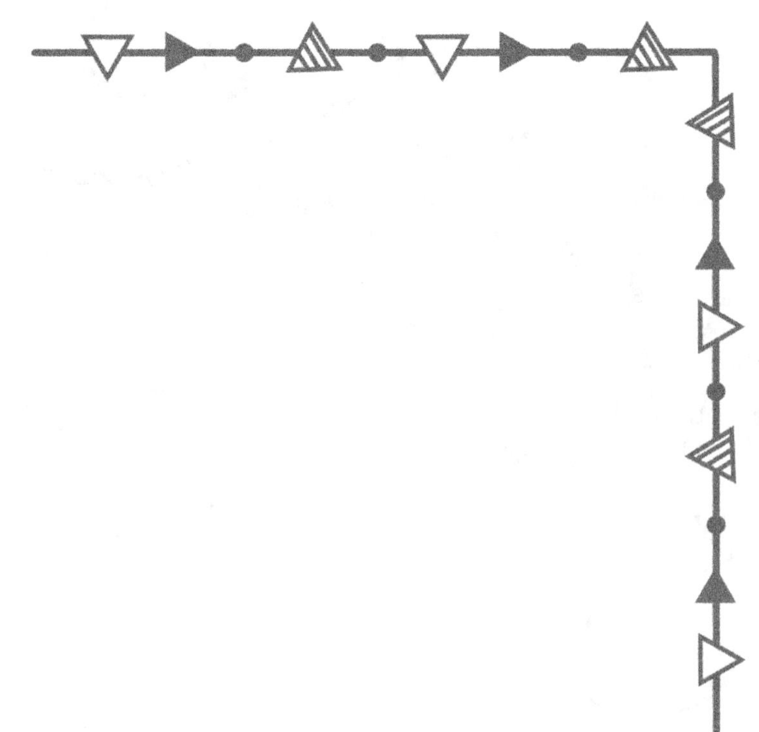

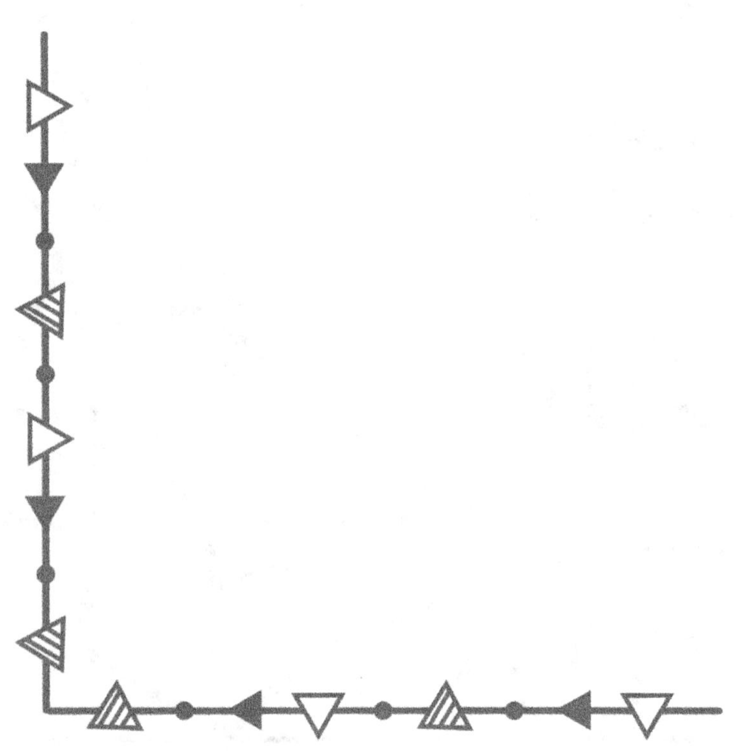

SLY
AS A
FOX

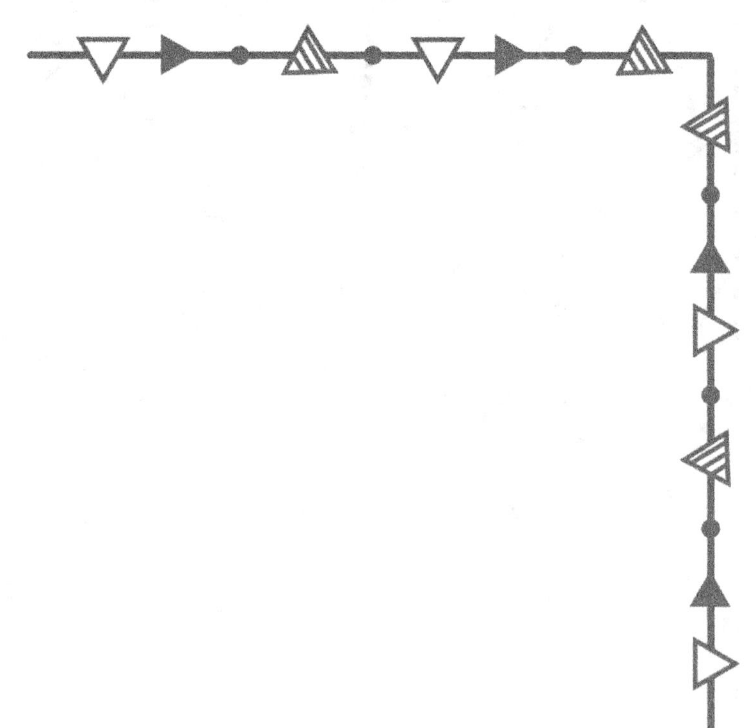
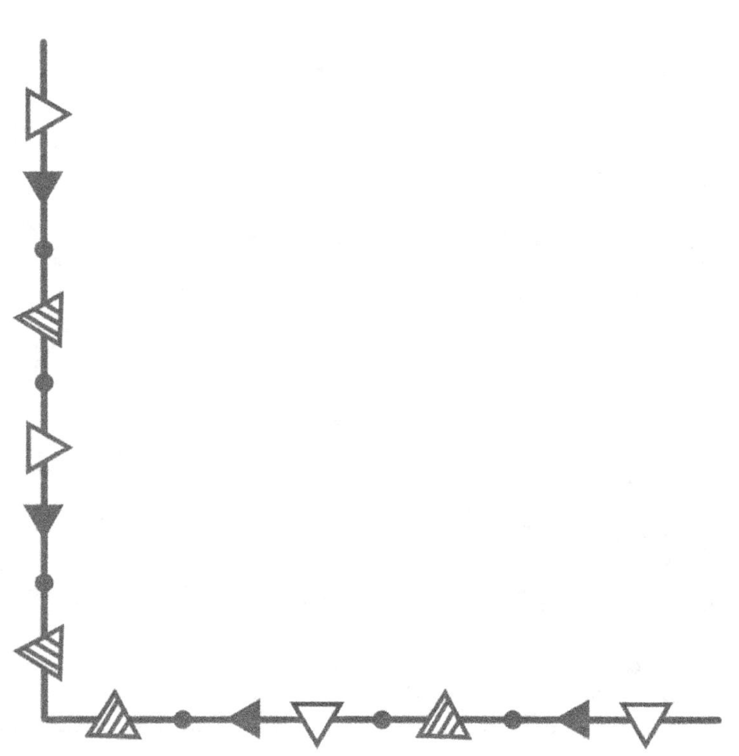

GRUMPY
as a
BEAR

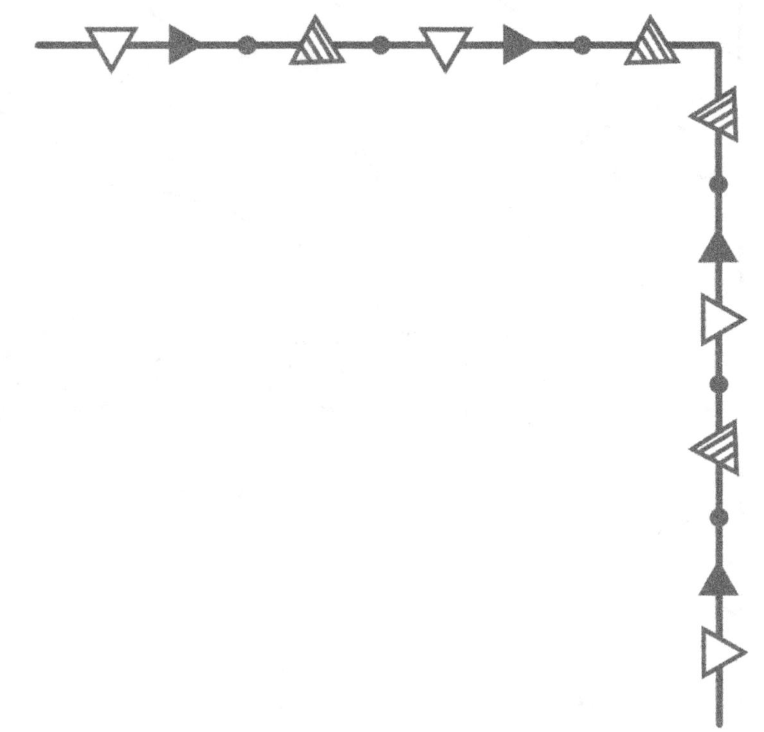

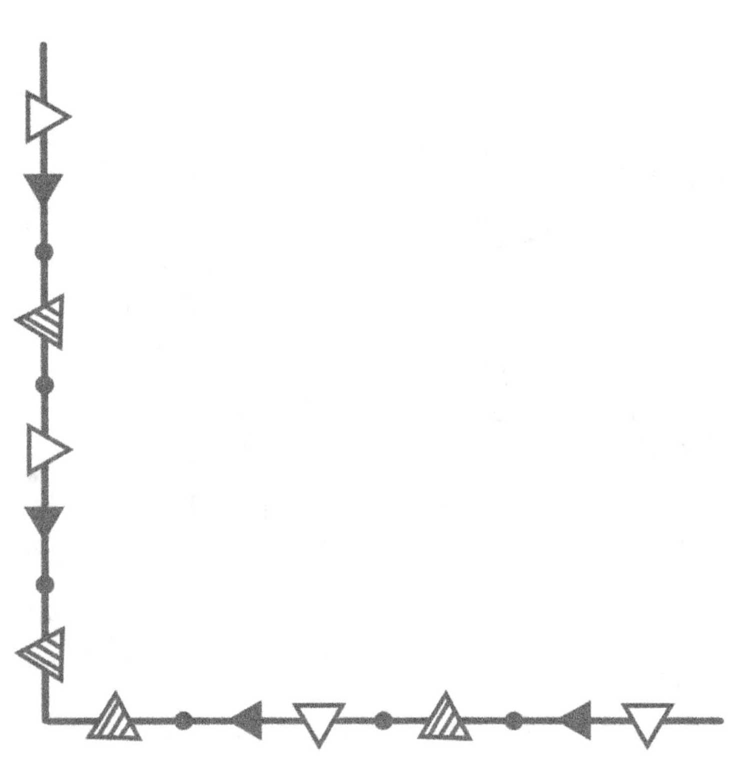

Graceful
as a
swan

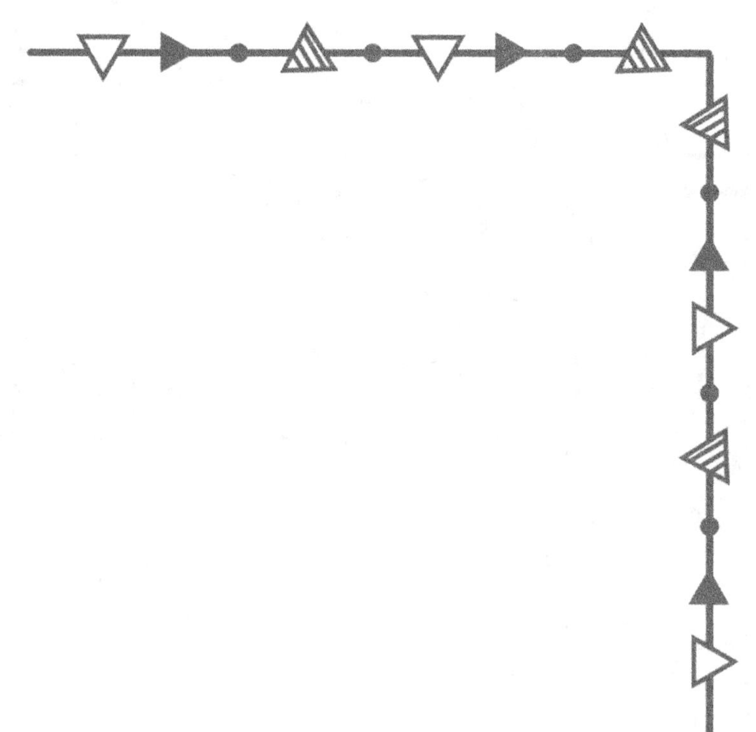
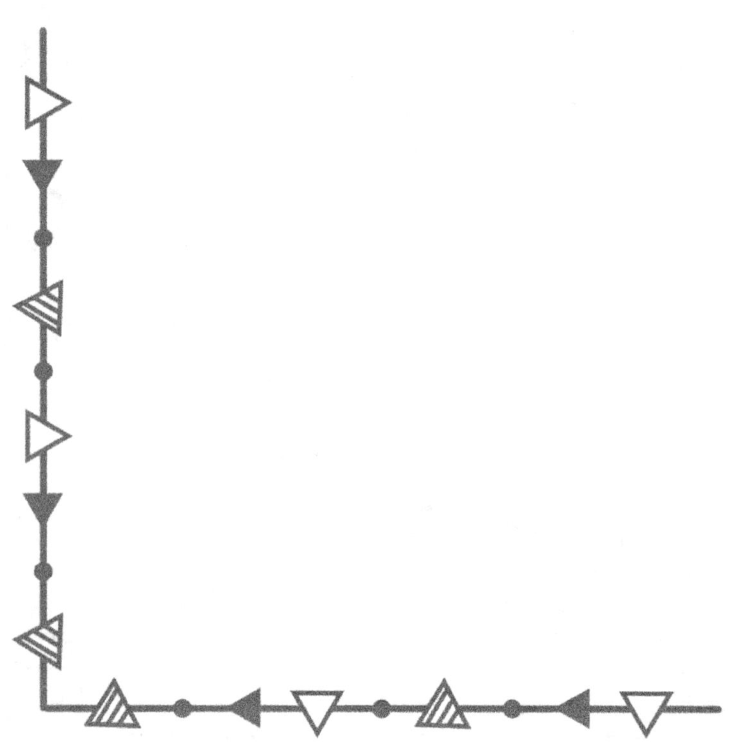

STUBBORN
as a
mule

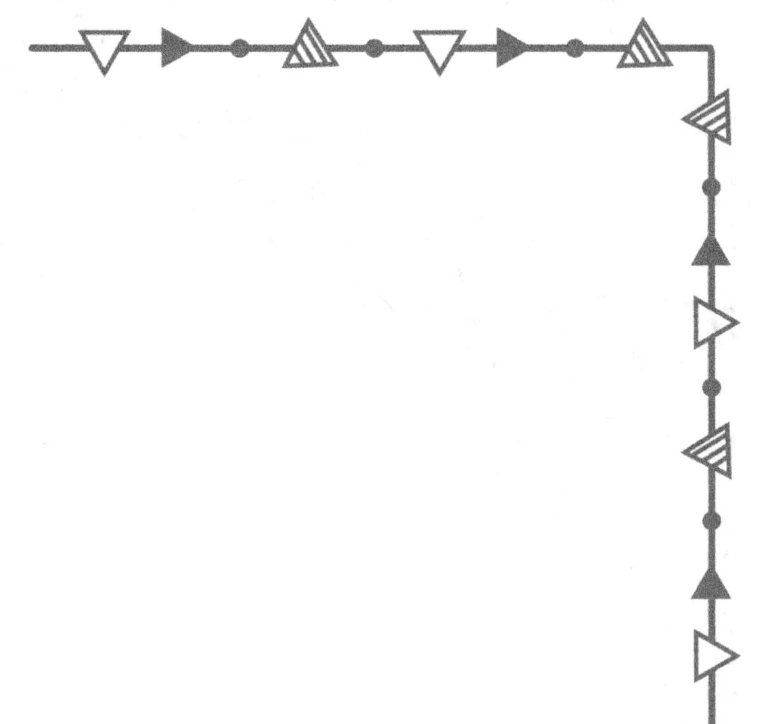
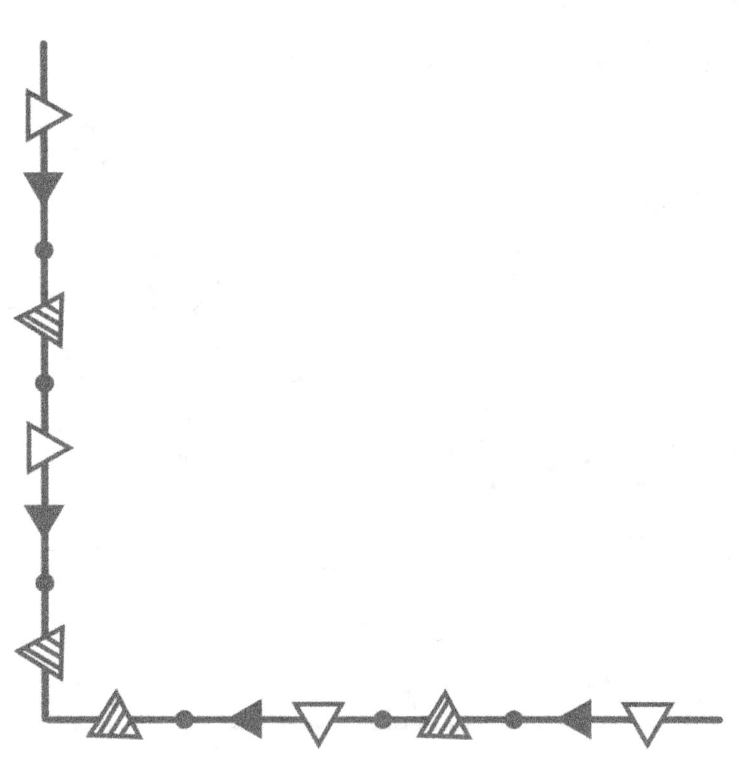

SLOW
as a
snail

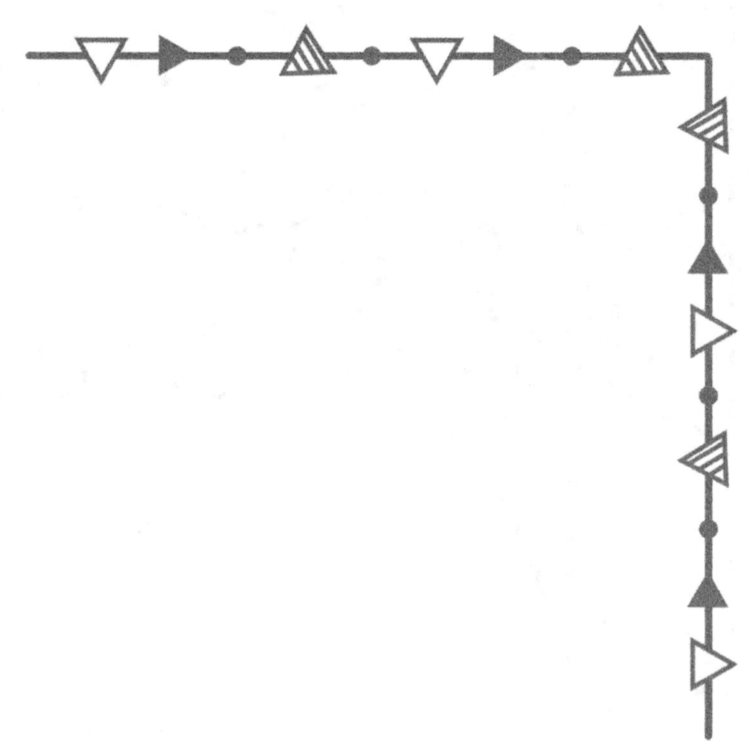
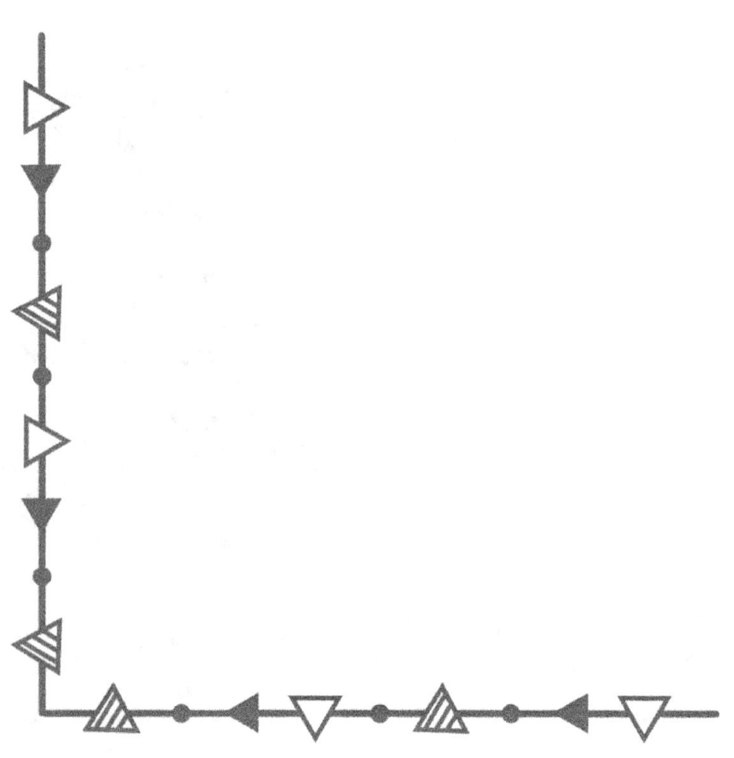

BiG
as an
elephant

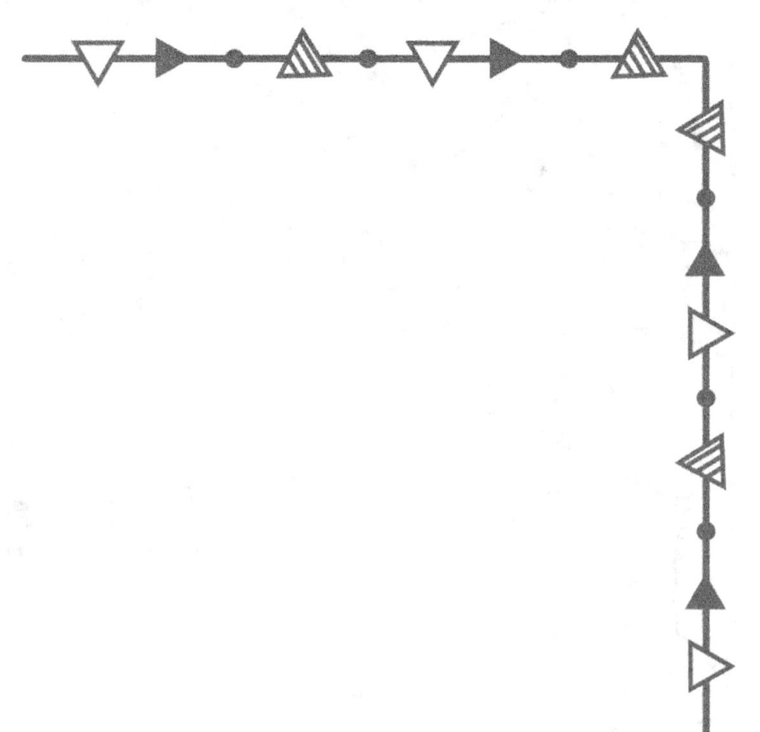
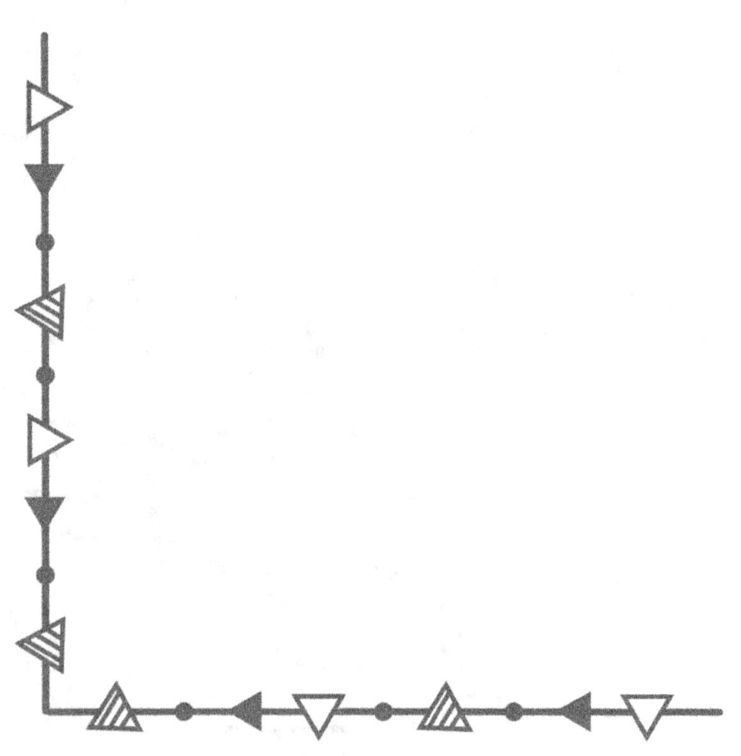

Quiet
as a
mouse

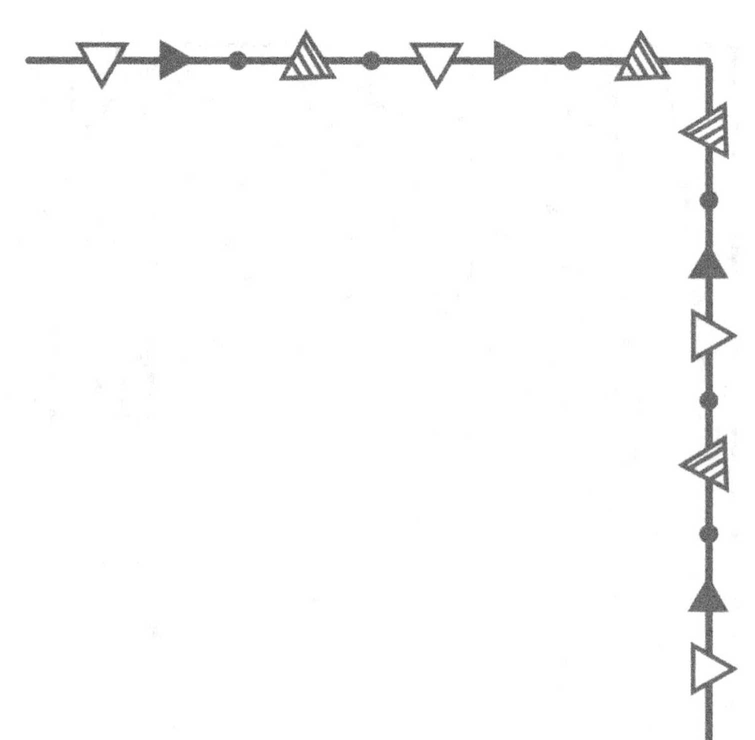

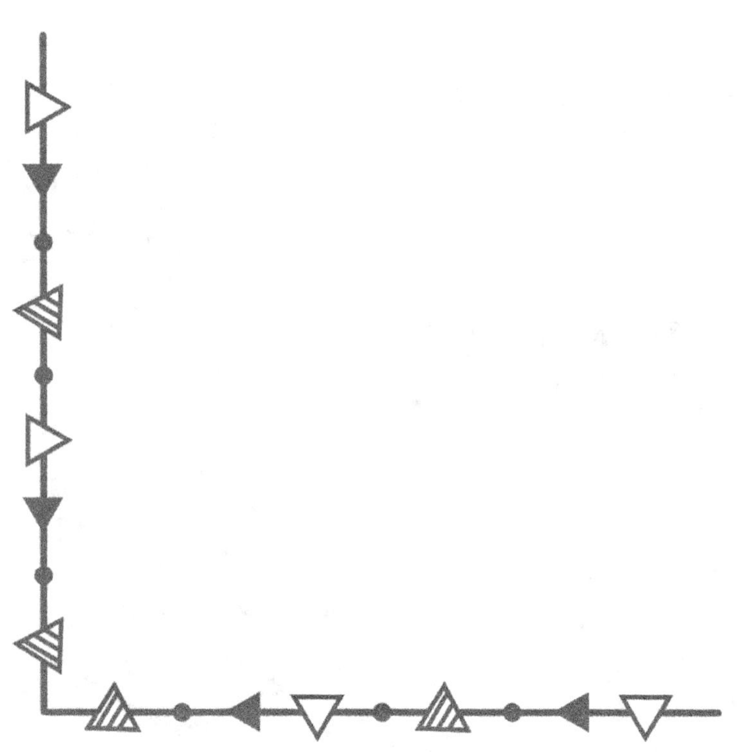

Funny
as a
Hyena

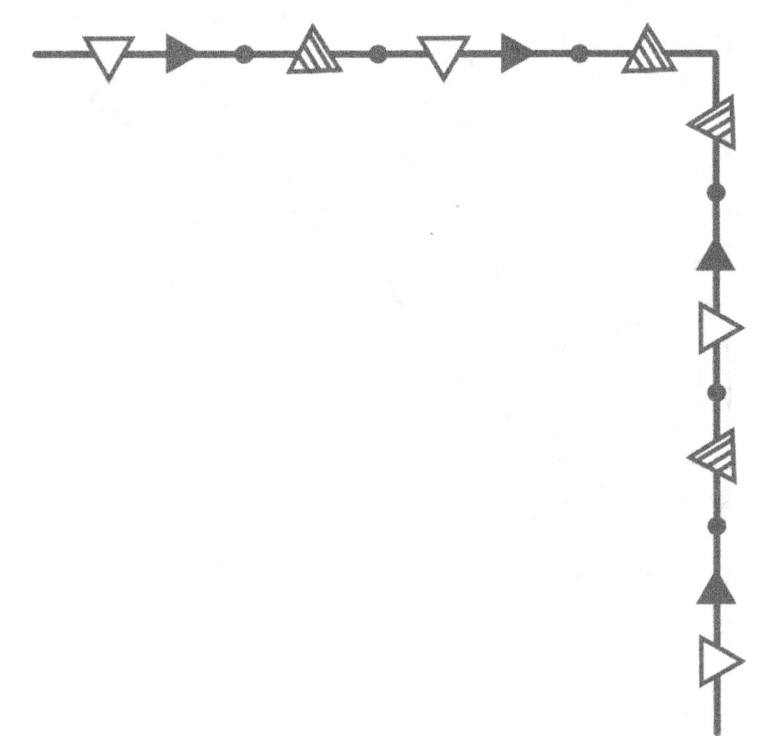
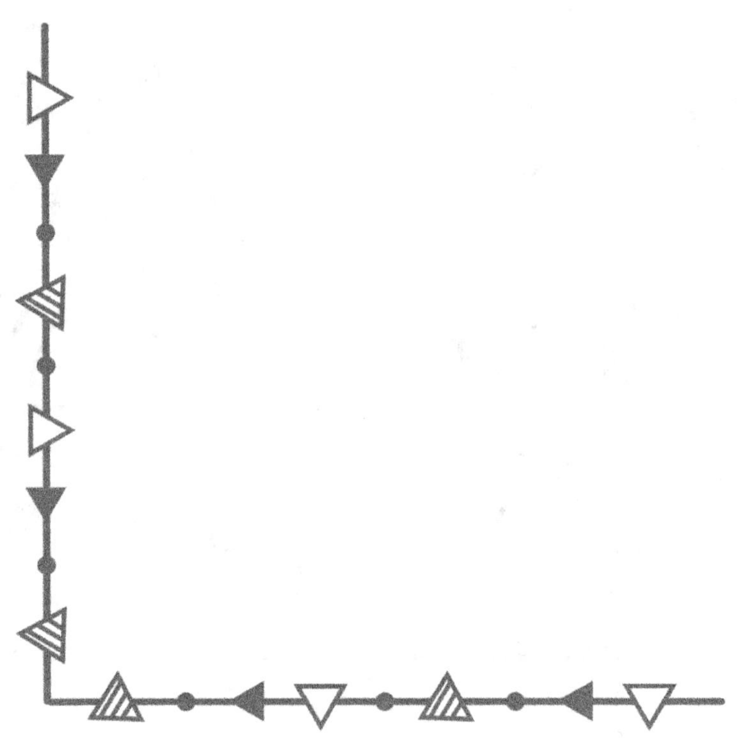

Fast
as a
Cheetah

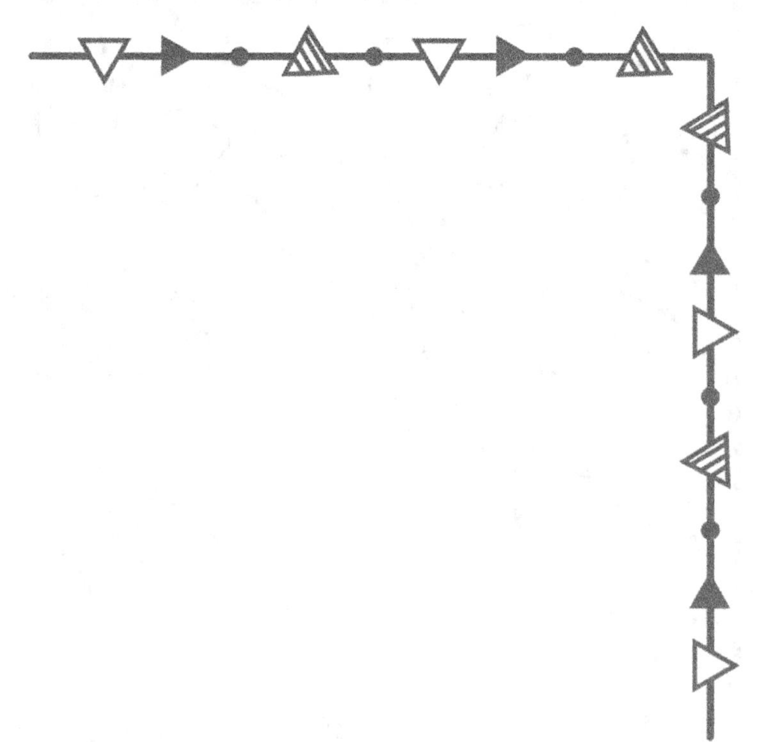
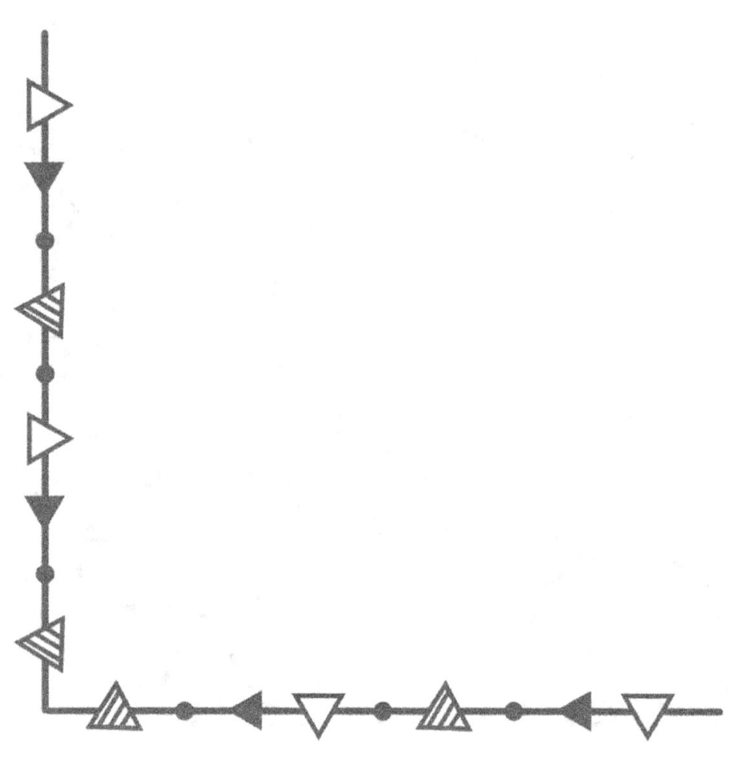

Busy
as a
Beaver

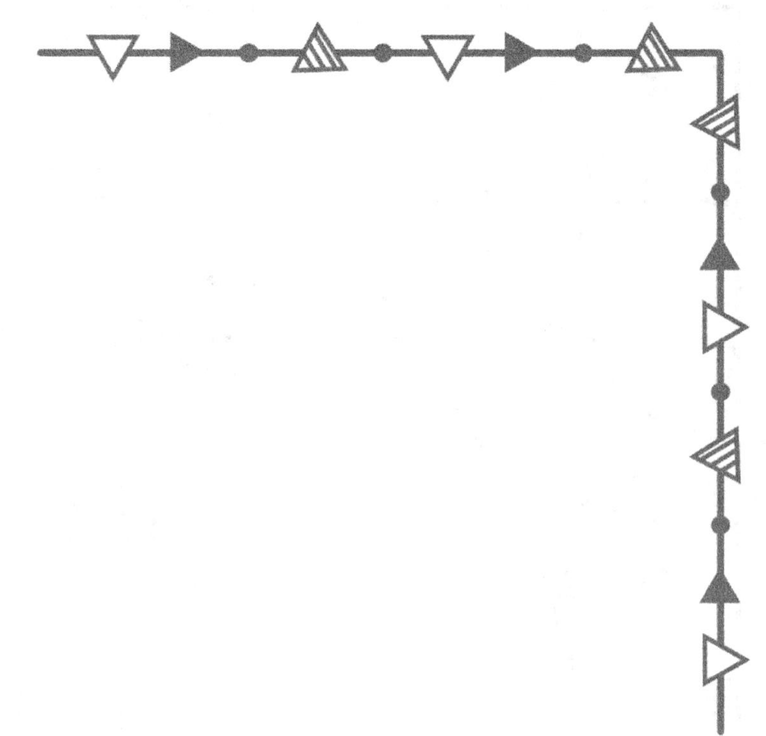
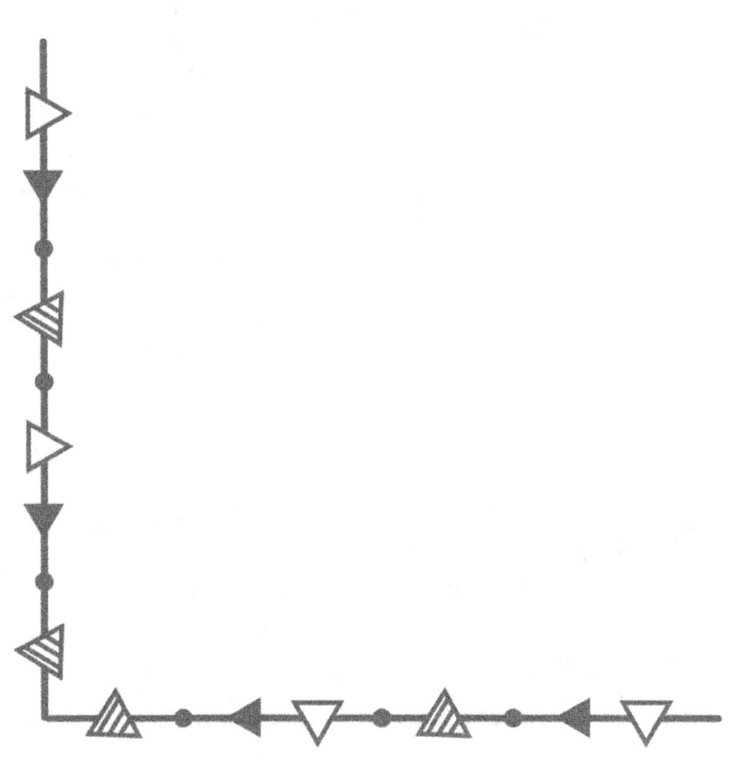

smelly
as a
skunk

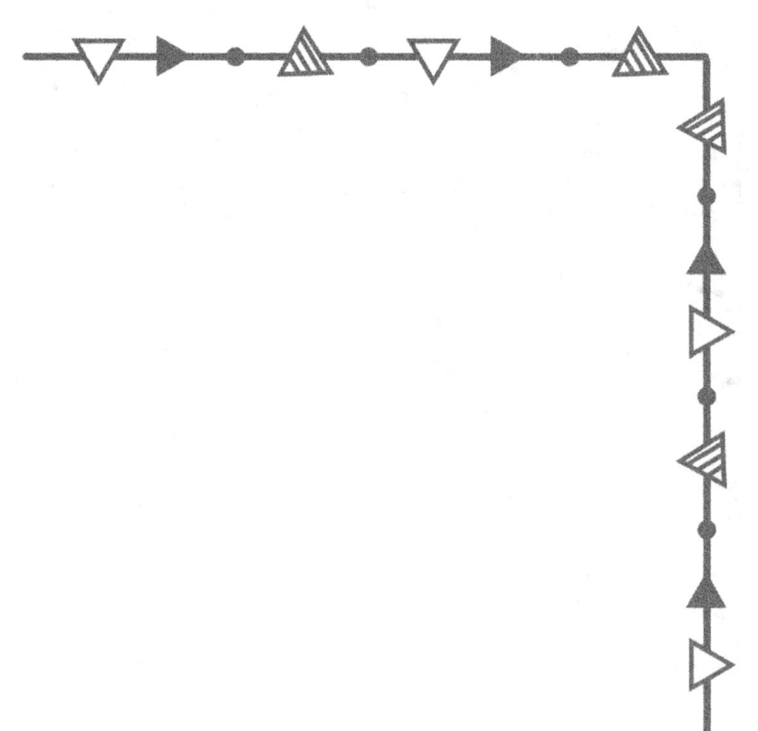
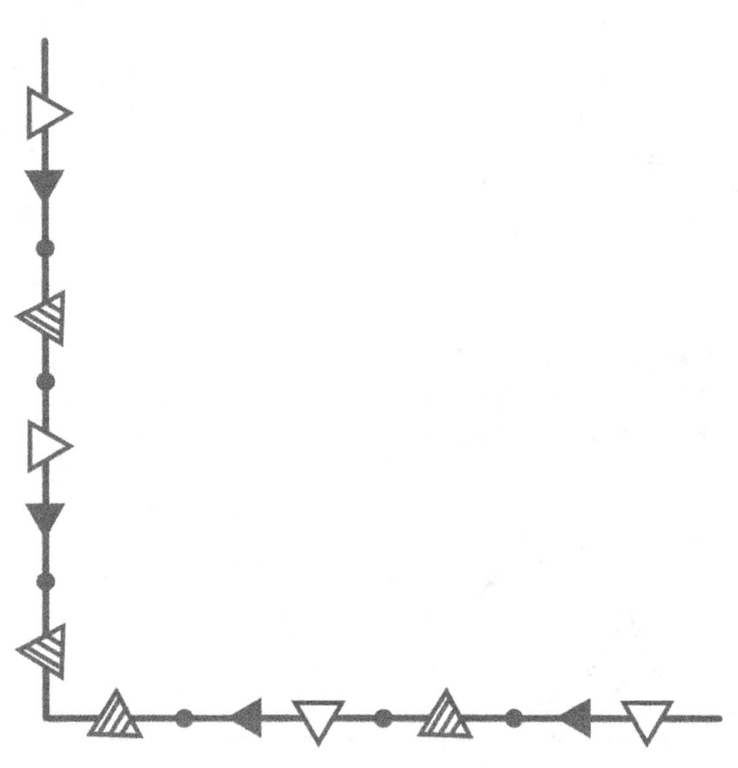

meek
as a
lamb

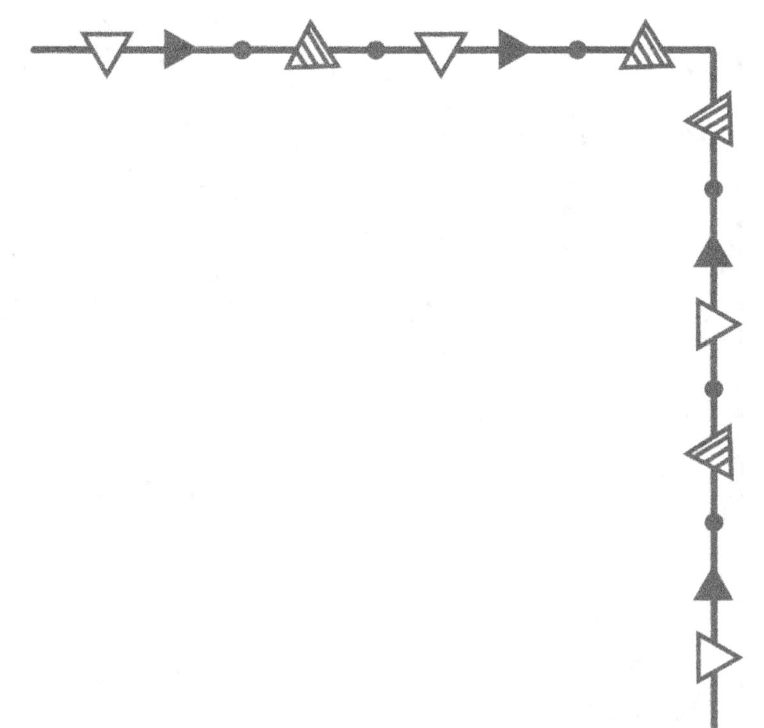
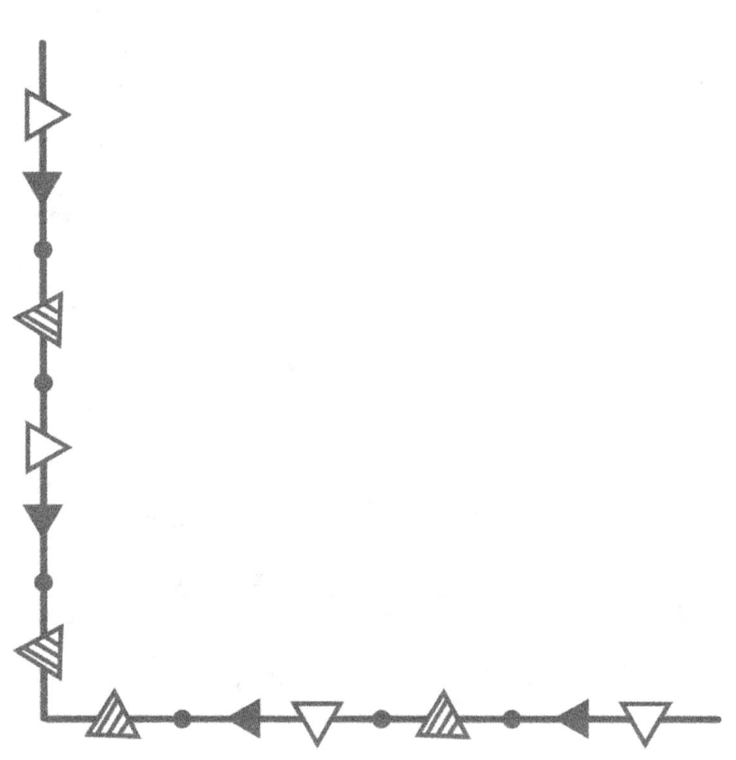

GREEDY
as a
PiG

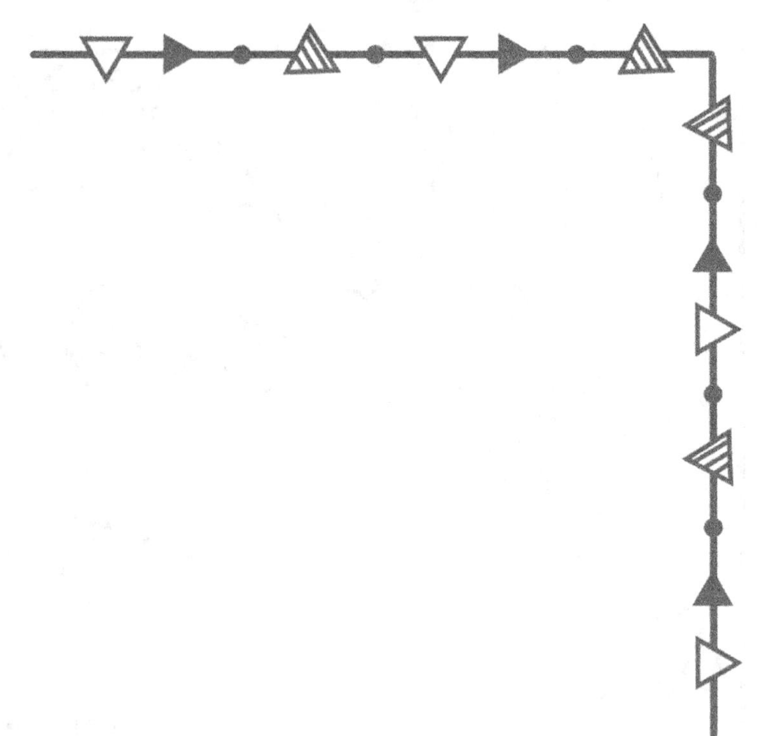
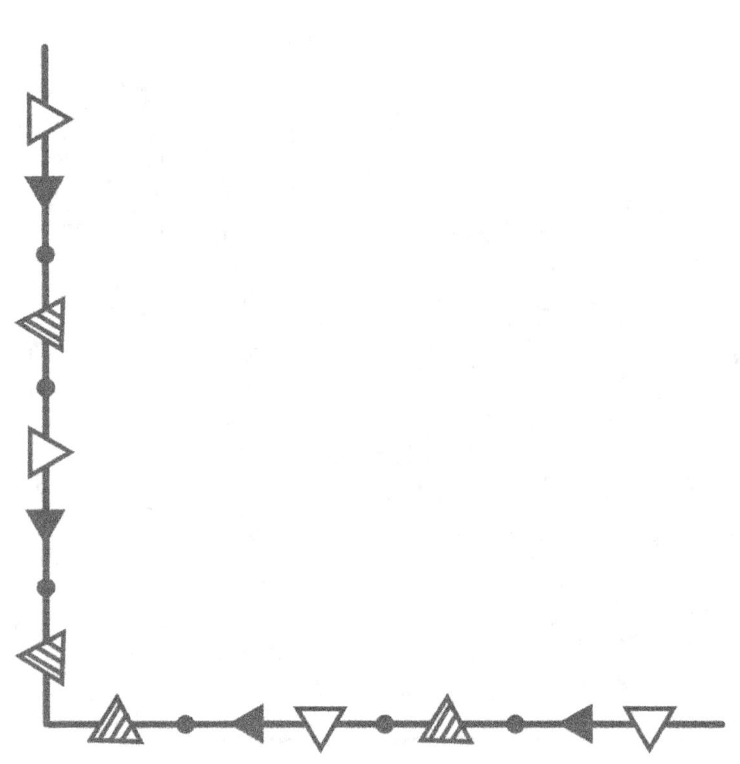

CUDDLY
AS A KOALA

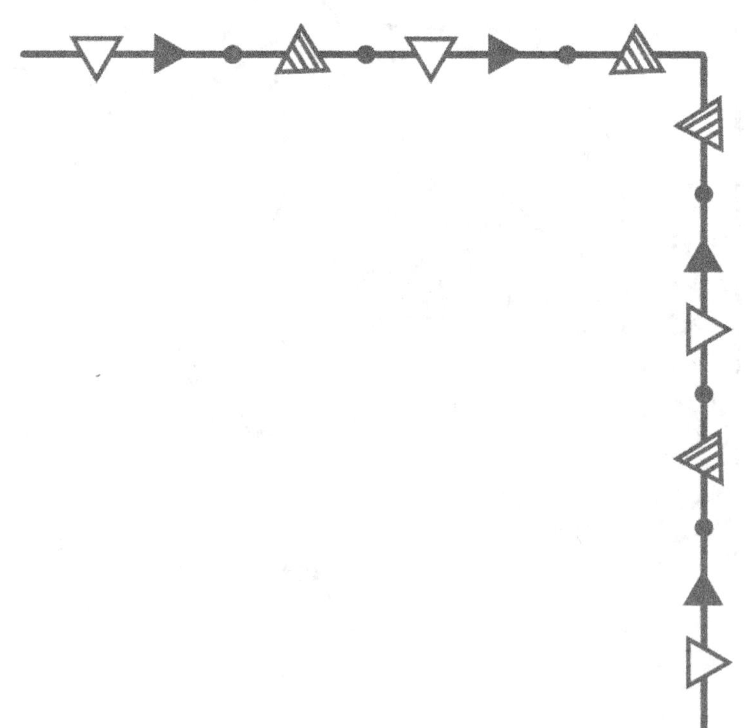
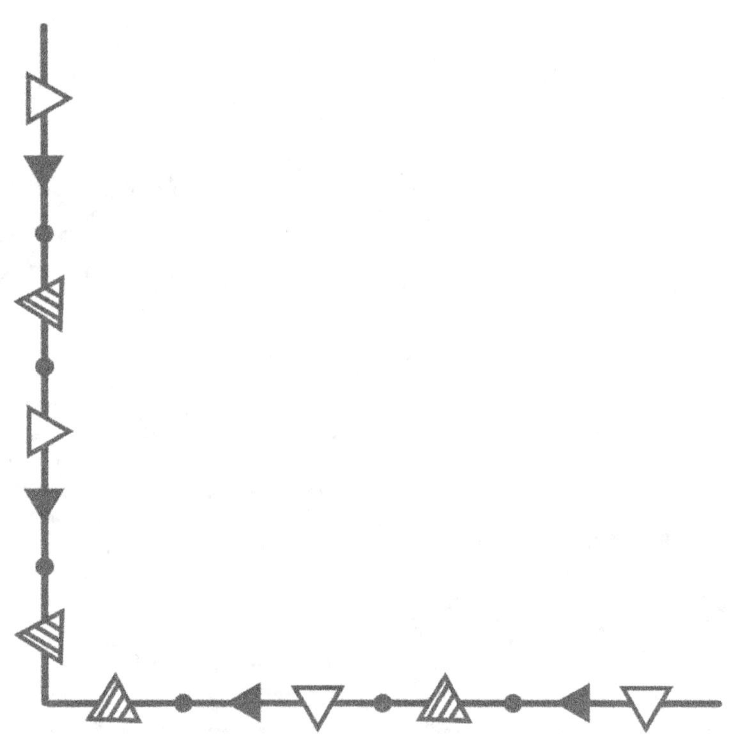

LOYAL
AS A
DOG

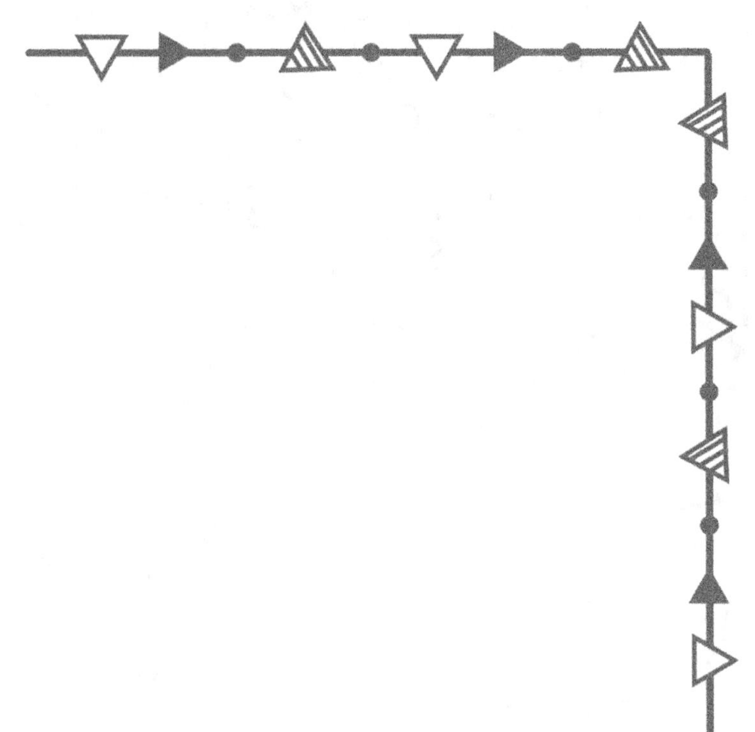

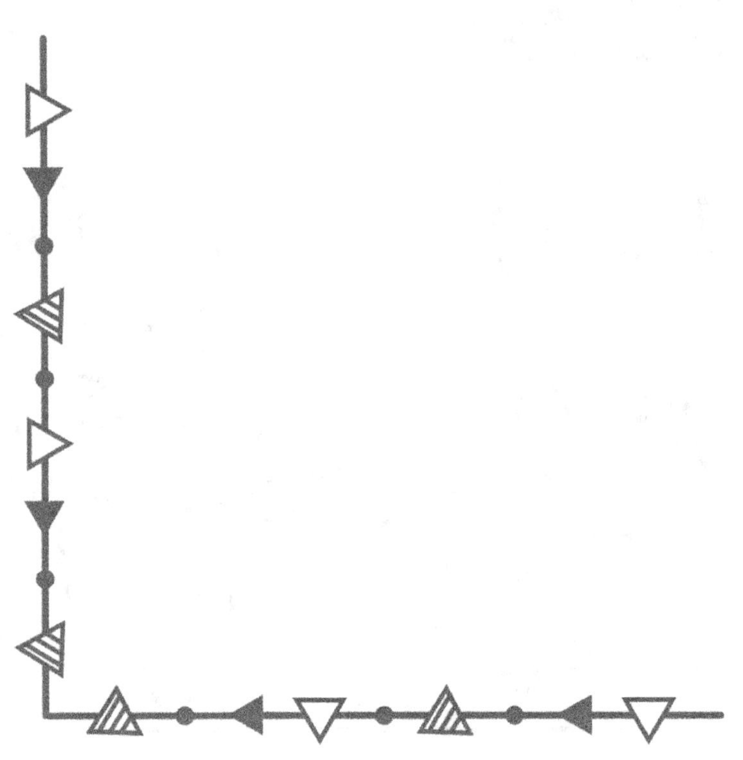

wise
as an owl

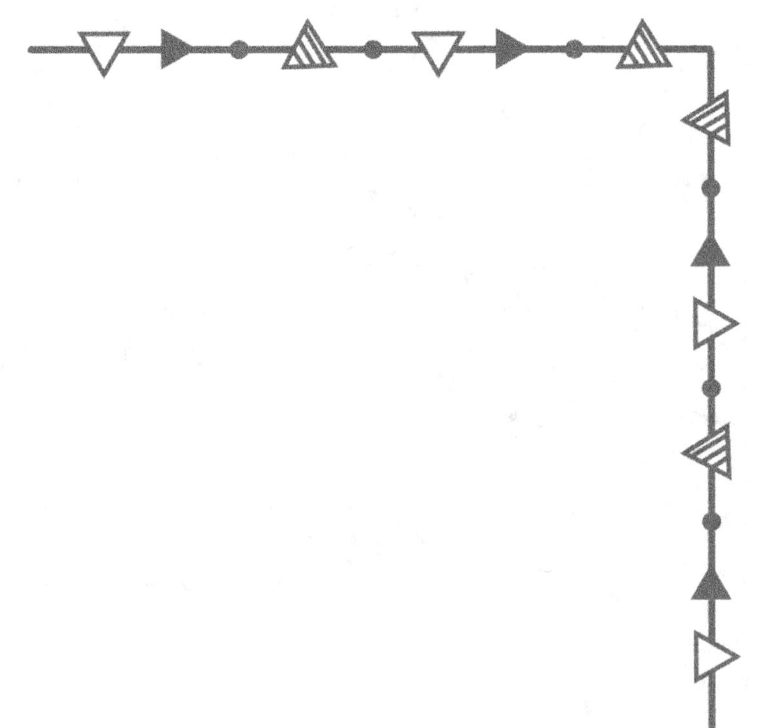
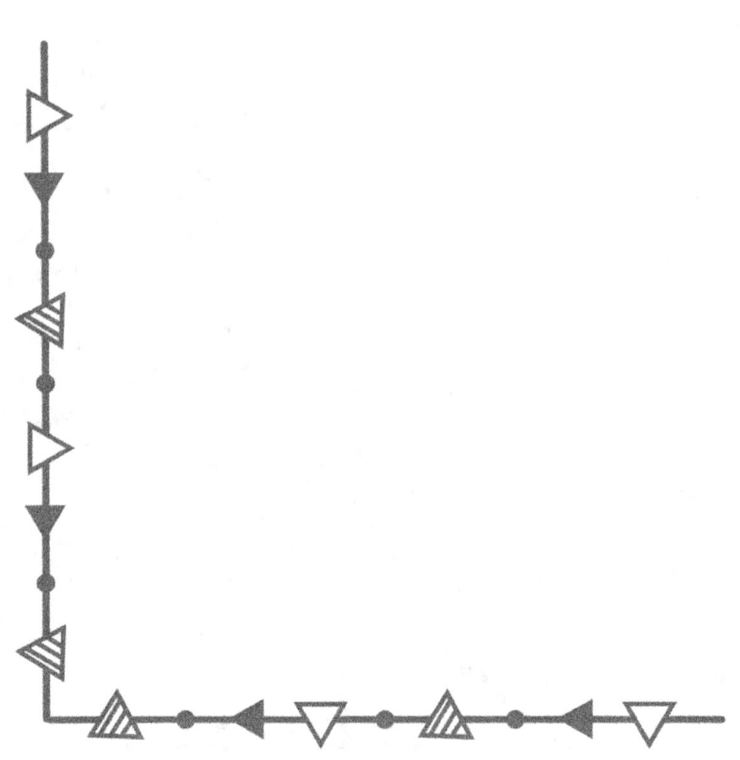

Blind
as a
Bat

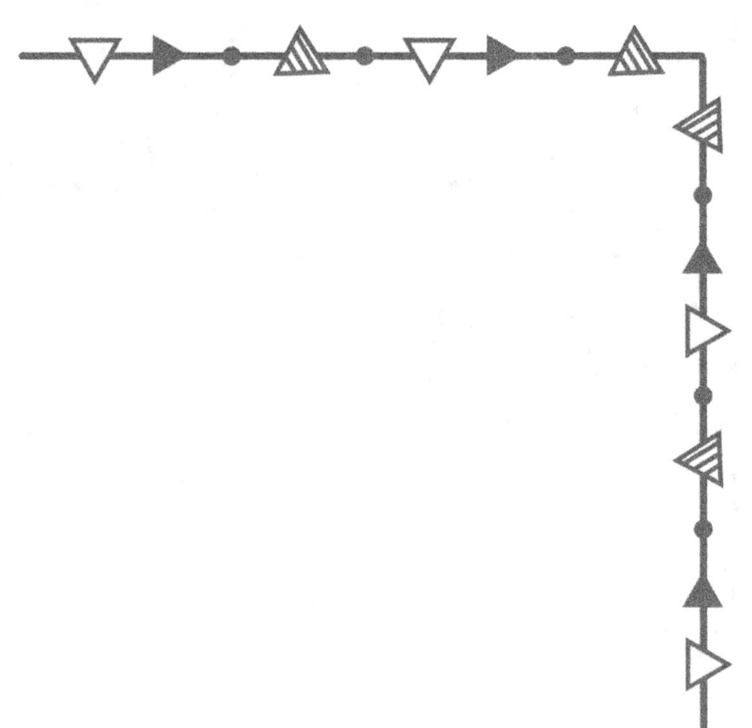
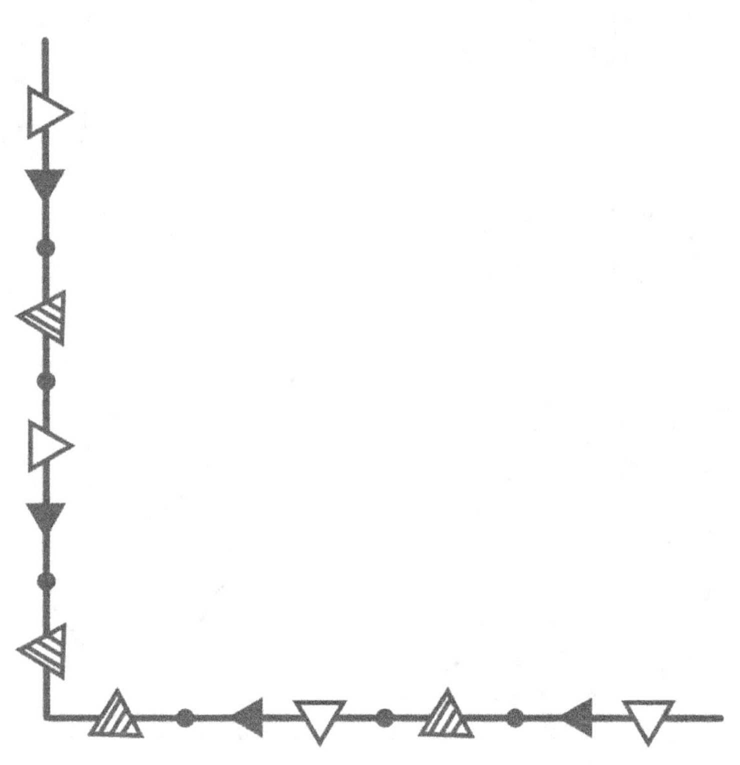

MEAN
as a
CROCODILE

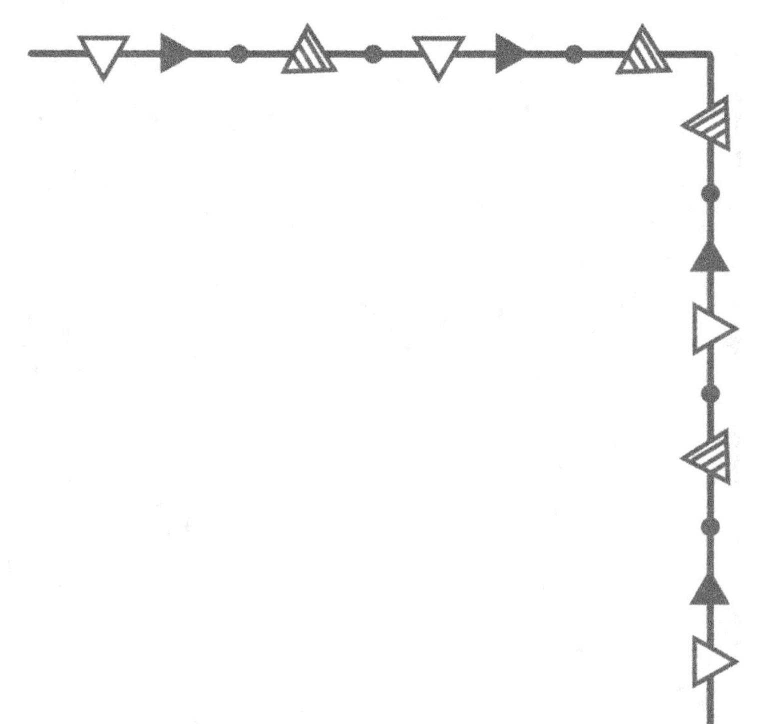
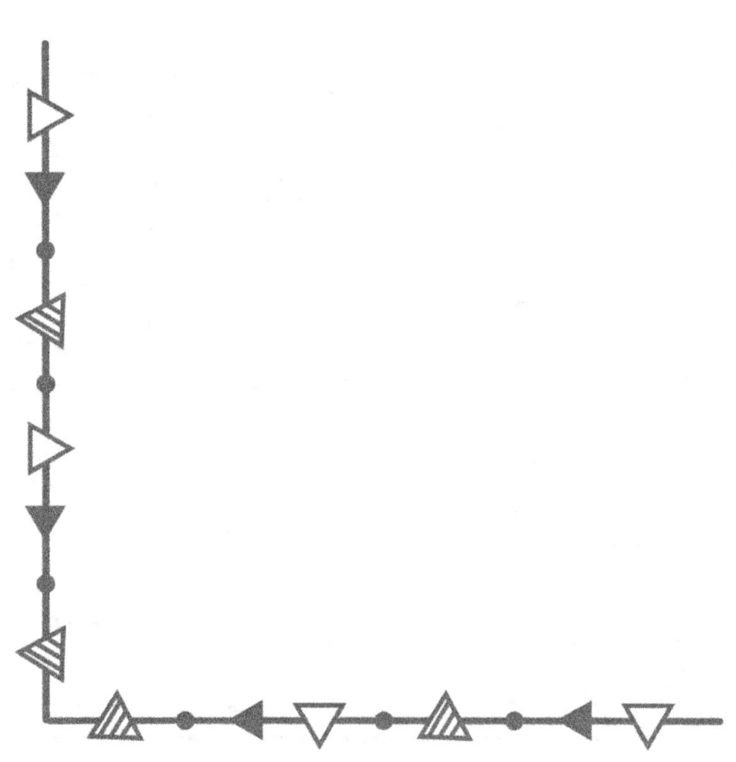

DUMB
AS AN OX

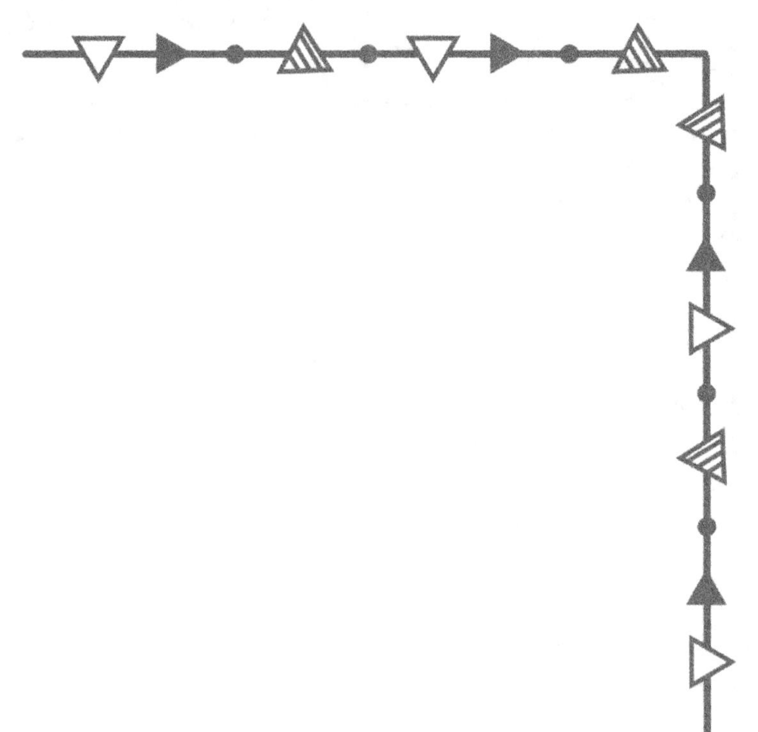
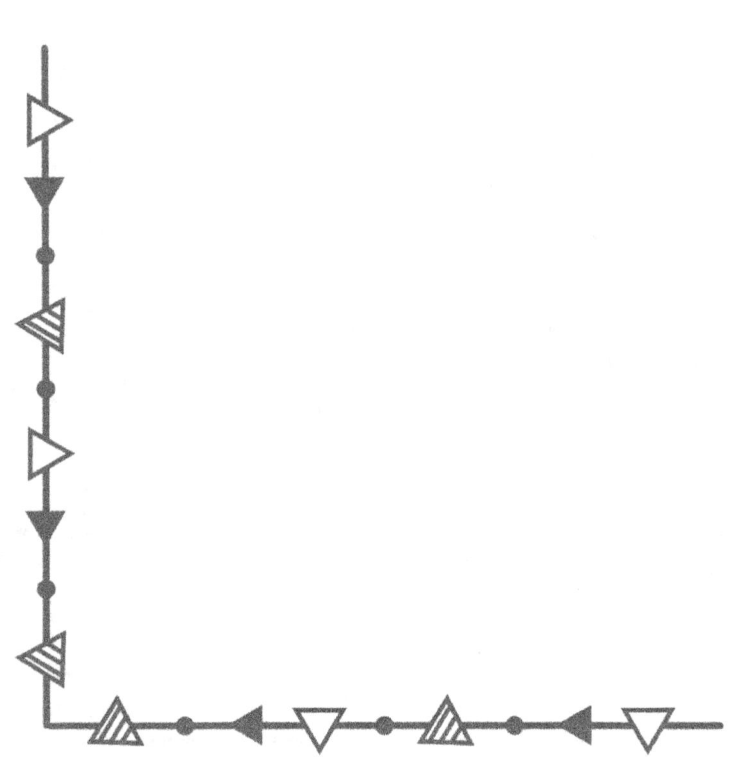

FLUFFY
as a
BUNNY

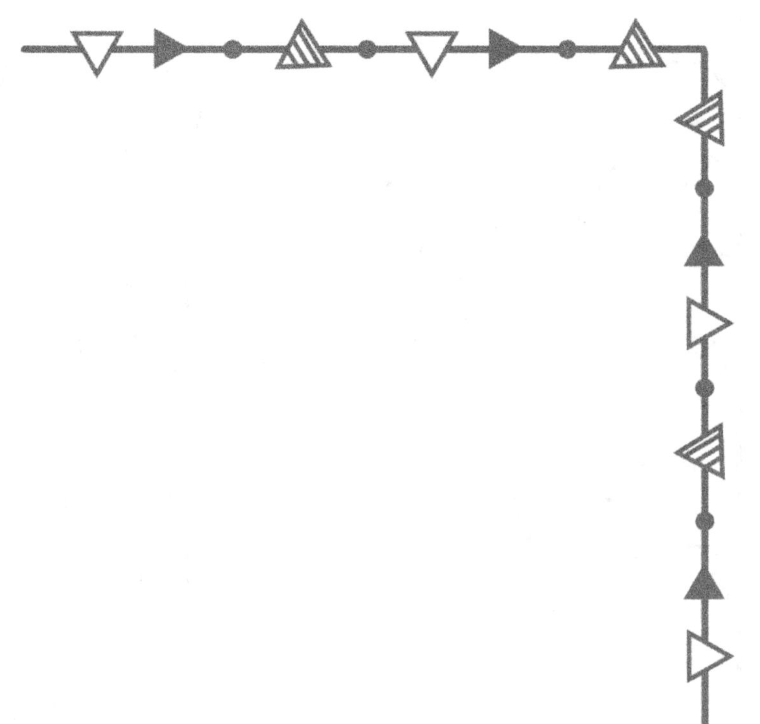
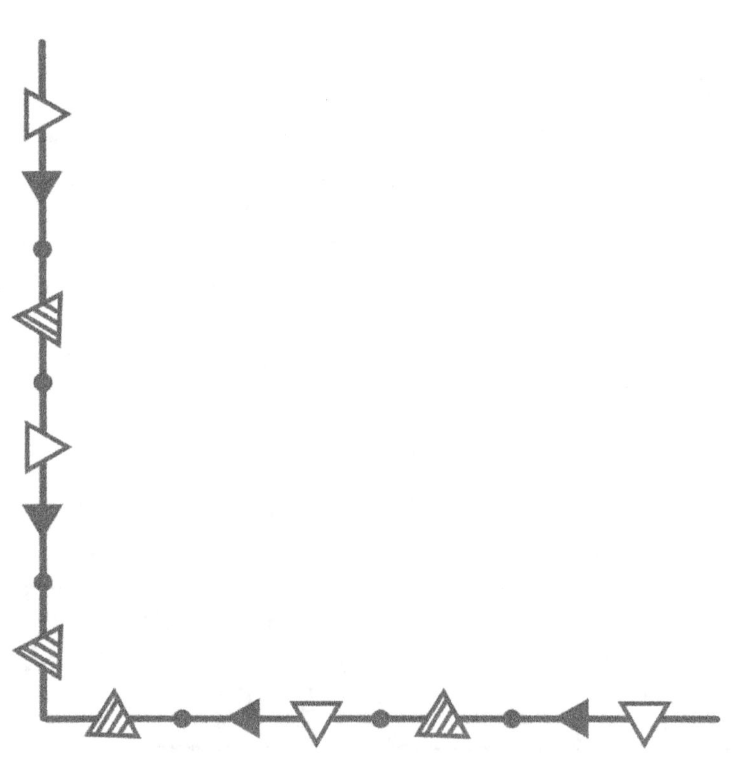

Busy
as a Bee

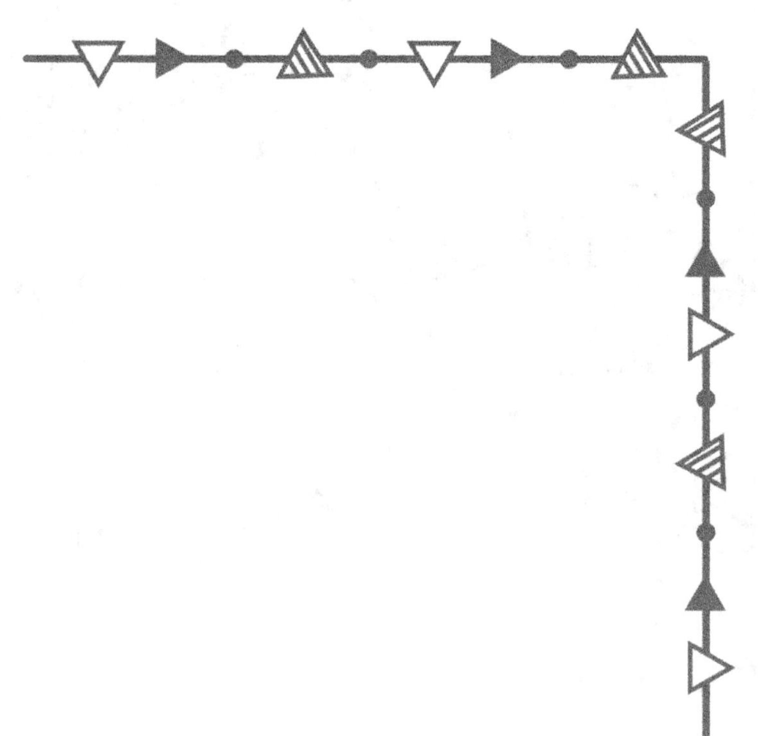
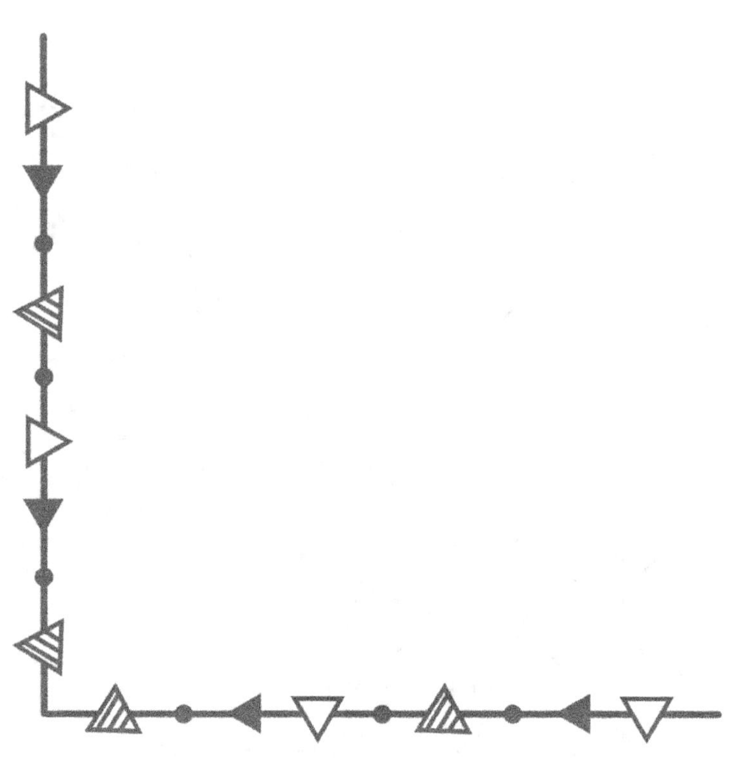

PRICKLY
as a
PORCUPINE

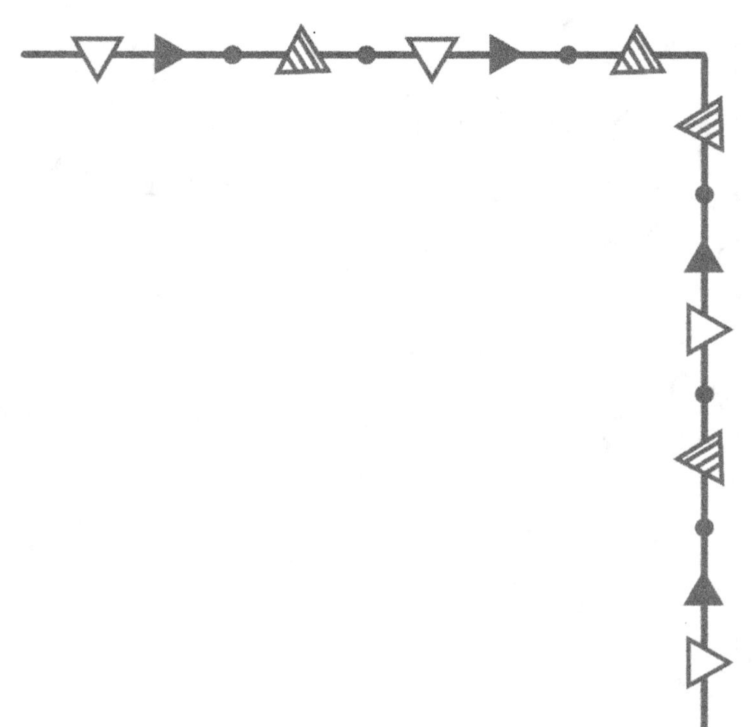
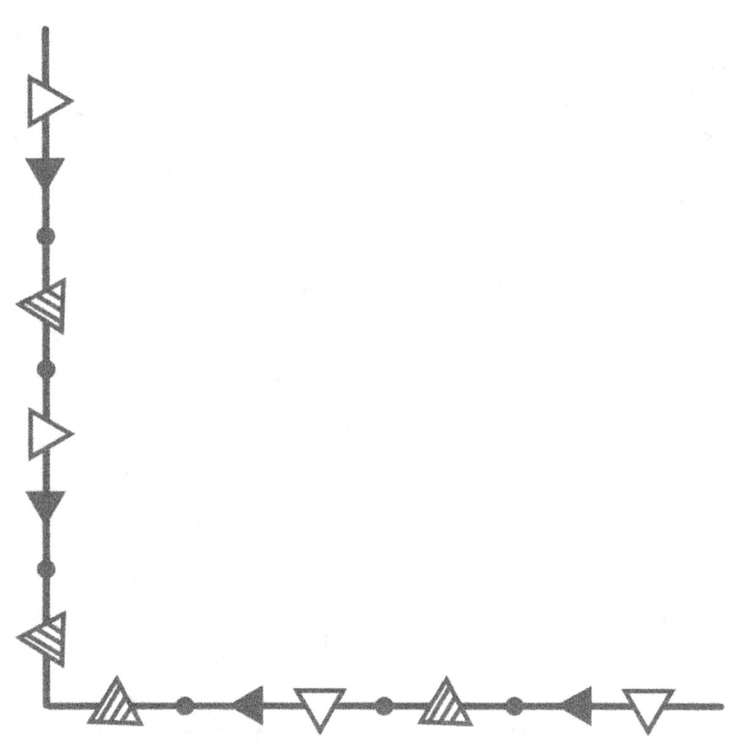

PROUD
AS A
LION

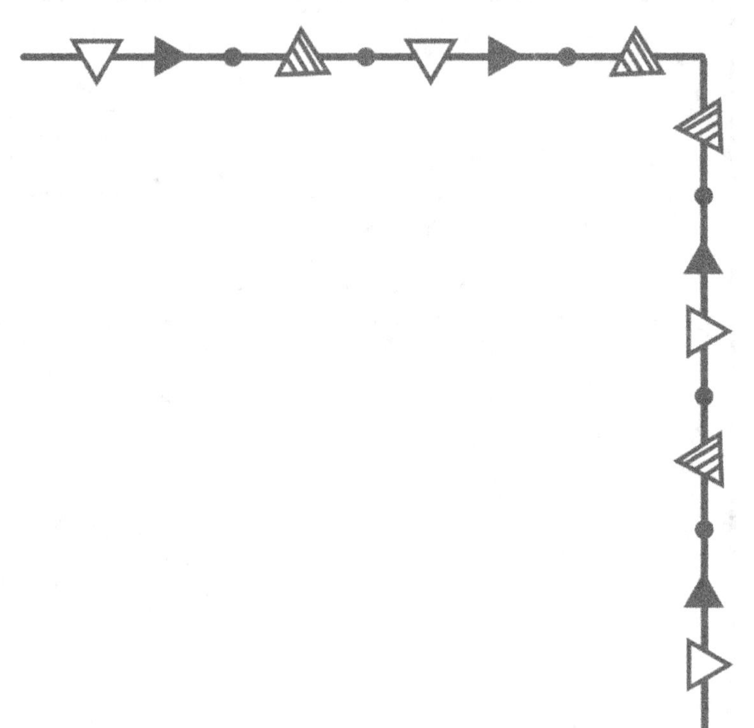
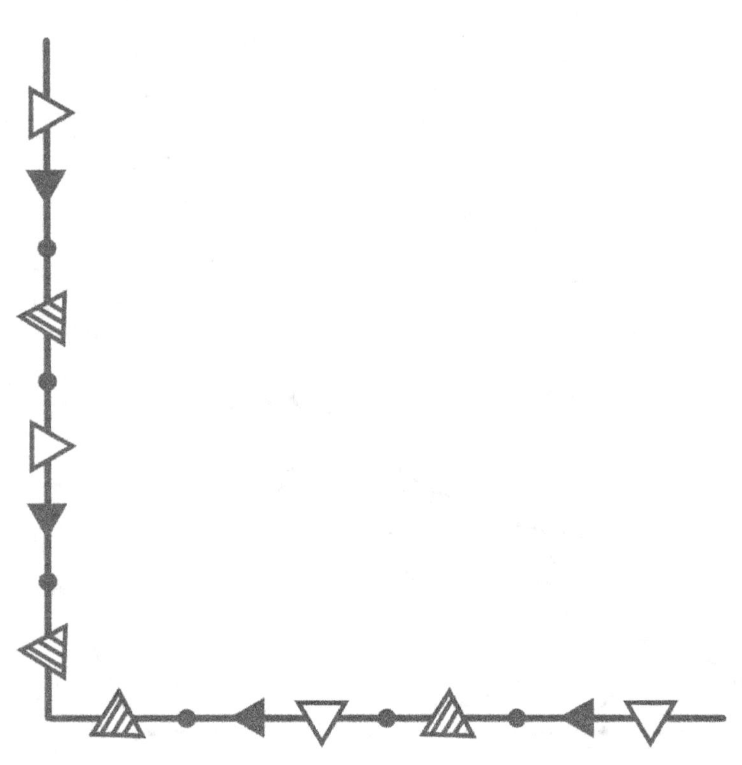

HUNGRY
as a
HIPPO

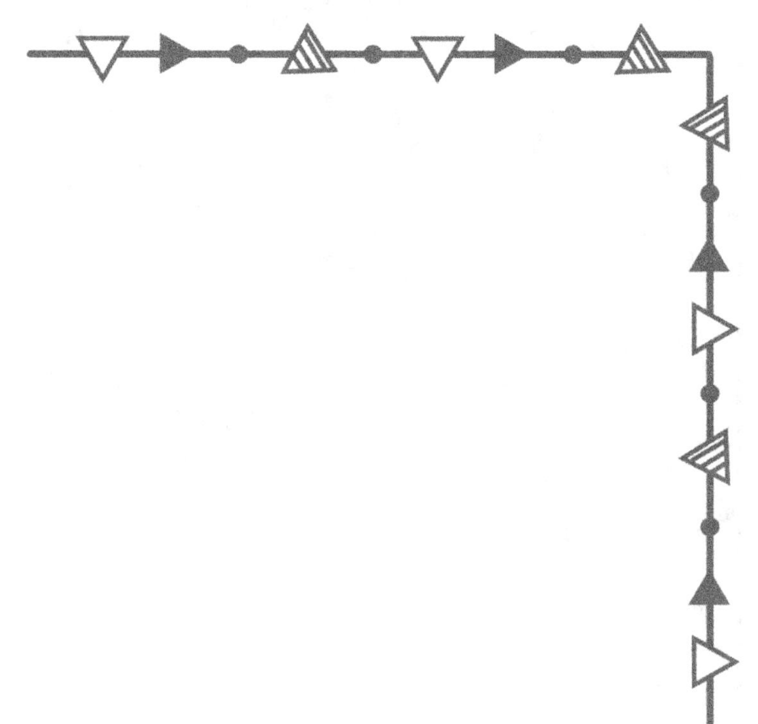
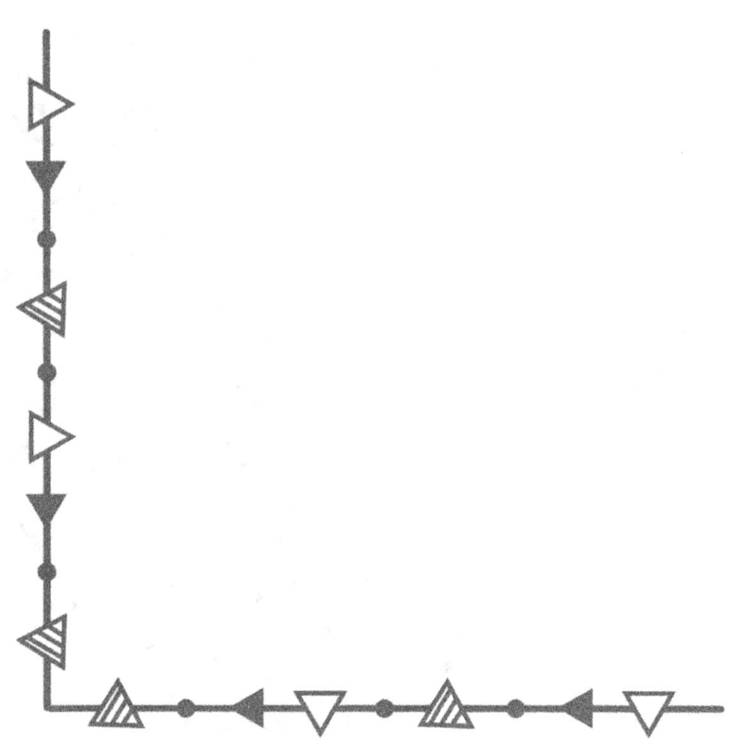

LAZY
AS A
SLOTH

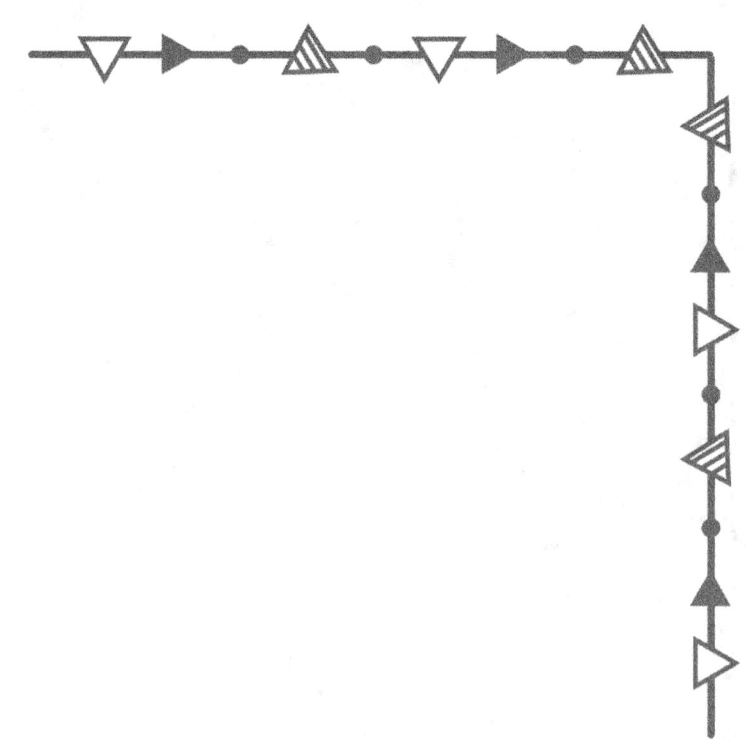
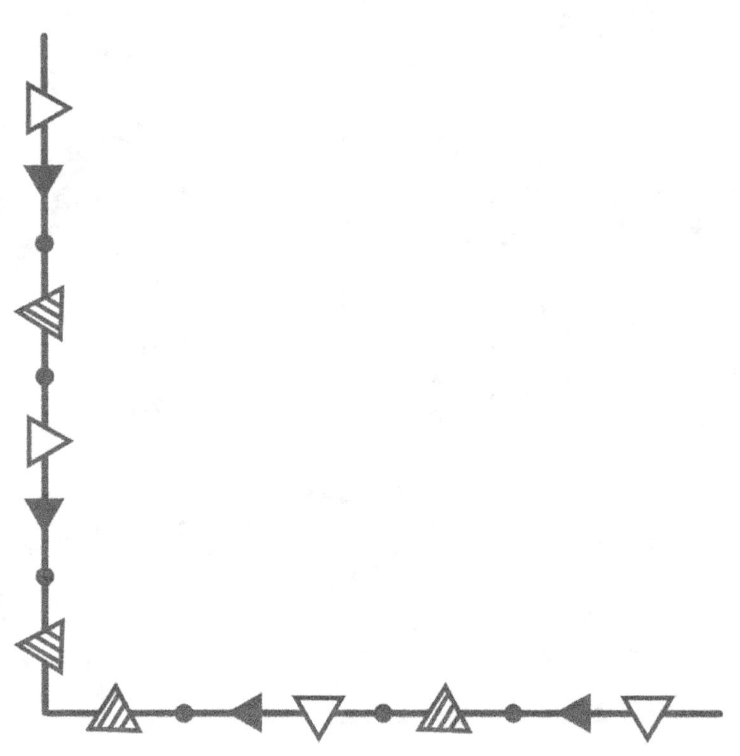

Test your Color Pencils & Gel Pens Below

Coloring Tip: Before coloring place a
blank sheet behind coloring page.
If necessary leave book page open to
dry before closing. Enjoy!

Test your Color Pencils & Gel Pens Below

Test your Color Pencils & Gel Pens Below

Test your Color Pencils & Gel Pens Below

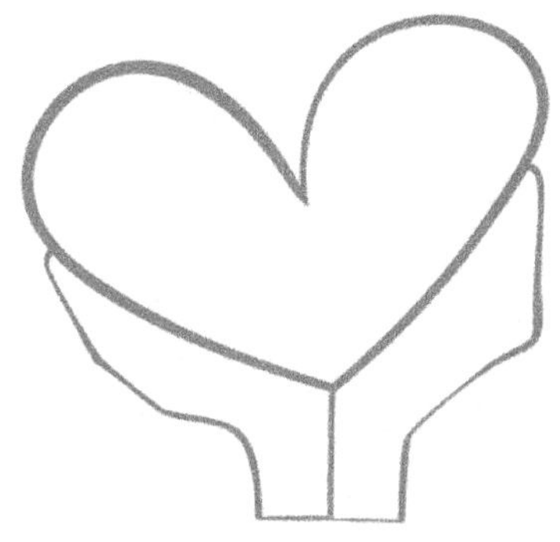

Thank you for purchasing this coloring book.

We would appreciate it, if you could give this book your opinion review. It really helps our small family business and we would enjoy hearing from you!

amazon.com/author/jillharmony

9 798726 933993